Learning and Applying SolidWorks 2008-2009 Step-by-Step

DISCARD

L. Scott Hansen, Ph.D.

Associate Professor of Engineering Technology
College of Computing, Integrated Engineering and Technology
Southern Utah University
Cedar City, Utah

Industrial Press, Inc
New York

ISBN 9780831133665

Third Edition, November 2008

Sponsoring Editor: John Carleo
Cover Design: Janet Romano

Industrial Press Inc.
989 Avenue of the Americas, 19th Floor
New York, NY 10018

10 9 8 7 6 5 4 3 2 1

Note to the Reader

This book provides clear and concise applied instruction in order to help you develop a mastery of *SolidWorks*. Almost every instruction includes a graphic illustration to aid in clarifying that instruction. Software commands appear in **bold** or in "quotation marks" for anyone who prefers not to read every word of the text. Most illustrations also include small pointer arrows and text to further clarify instructions.

This book was written for classroom instruction or self-study, including for individuals with no solid modeling experience at all. You will begin at a very basic level, but by the time you finish you will be completing complex functions.

For any organization requiring additional help, I am available for onsite training. Please contact me at hansens@suu.edu

Scott Hansen
Cedar City, Utah

Table of Contents

Chapter 1 Getting Started

Objectives:

- Create a simple sketch using the Sketch commands
- Dimension a sketch using the Smart Dimension command
- Extrude a sketch using the Extruded Boss/Base command
- Create a hole using the Extrude Cut command
- Create a fillet using the Fillet command
- Create a counter bore using the Hole Wizard

Chapter 1 includes instruction on how to design the part shown below.

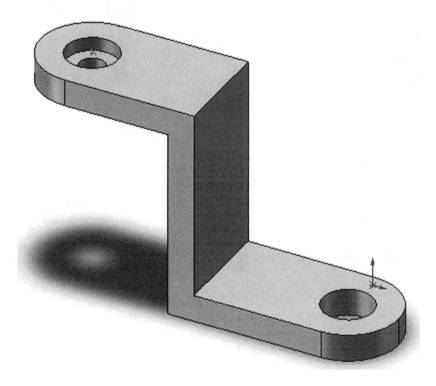

1.   Start SolidWorks by moving the cursor to the button in the lower left corner of the screen. Click the left mouse button once.

2.   A pop up menu of the programs that are installed on the computer will appear. Scroll through the list of programs until you find "SolidWorks".

3.   Move the cursor over the text "SolidWorks" and left click once as shown in Figure 1.

Figure 1

4.   SolidWorks will open (load up and begin running).

5.   Move the cursor to the upper left corner of the screen and left click on the "New Document" icon as shown in Figure 2.

Figure 2

6. The New SolidWorks Document dialog box will appear. Left click on **Part** as shown in Figure 3.

Figure 3

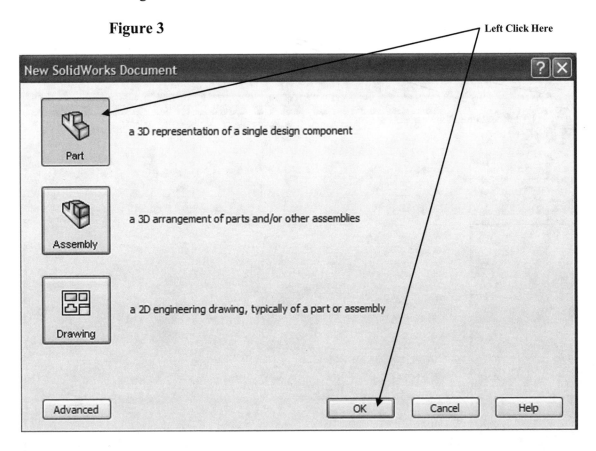

7. Left click on **OK**.

8. The screen should look similar to Figure 4. Left click on **Sketch**. If the Sketch tools are not visible, left click on the **Sketch** tab as shown.

Figure 4

Left Click Here

9. SolidWorks will display three different work planes. Move the cursor over the "Front Plane" until it turns red. Left click once as shown in Figure 5. SolidWorks will provide a perpendicular view of the front plane.

Figure 5

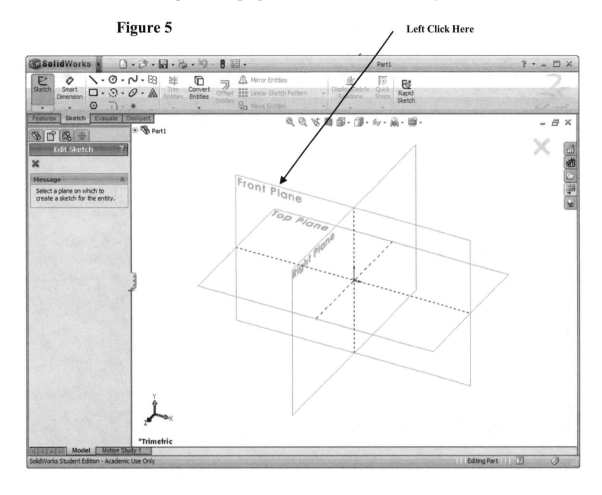

10. Your screen should look similar to Figure 6.

Figure 6

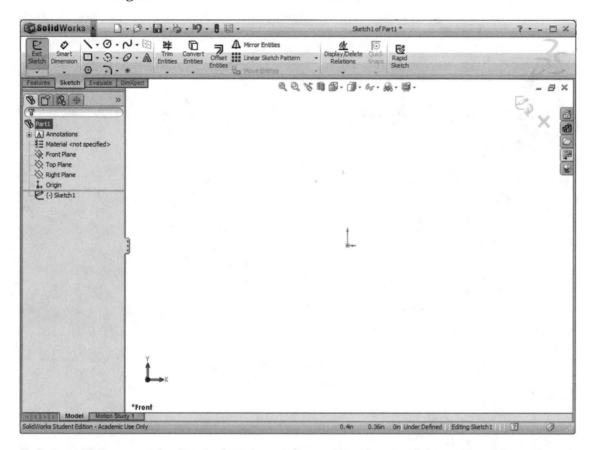

11. If the grid is displayed, skip to instruction number 12. If there is no grid visible, continue following the next steps.

NOTE: Move the cursor to the upper left portion of the screen and left click on the arrow to the right of SolidWorks (the arrow will facing to the right). Left click on **Tools** as shown in Figure A.

Figure A

A drop down menu will appear. Left click on **Options** as shown in Figure B.

Figure B

The Document Properties - Detailing dialog box will appear. Left click on the **Document Properties** tab at the upper left portion of the dialog box as shown in Figure C.

Figure C

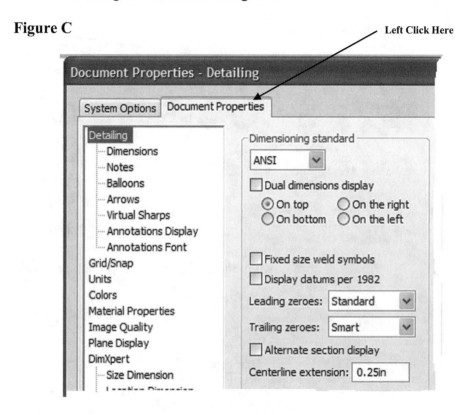

Move the cursor down to **Grid/Snap** and left click once. The Grid/Snap Properties will appear. Place a check in the box (with the left mouse button) next to Display Grid as shown in Figure D. To change drawings units, (not shown) left click on **Units** and place a dot to the left of (IPS), inch pound, second.

Figure D

Left click on **OK** as shown in Figure E.

Figure E

Left Click Here

SolidWorks should now display a visible grid as shown in Figure F.

Figure F

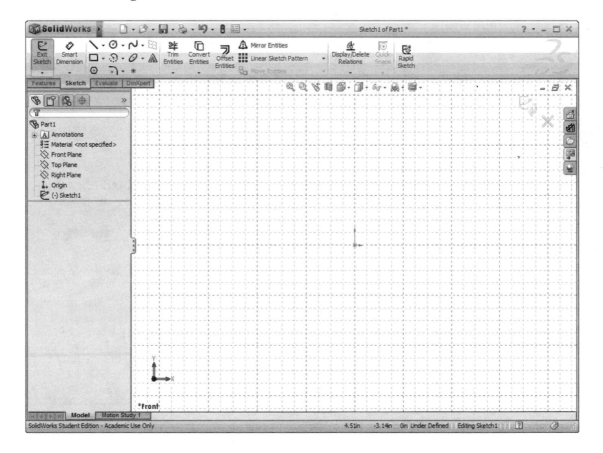

12. SolidWorks is now ready for use. Left click on **Line** as shown in Figure 7.

Figure 7

Left Click Here

13. Move the cursor in the lower left portion of the screen and left click once. This will be the beginning end point of a line as shown in Figure 8.

Figure 8

Left Click Here

0.25

14. Move the cursor towards the lower right portion of the screen and left click once as shown in Figure 9.

Figure 9

Left Click Here

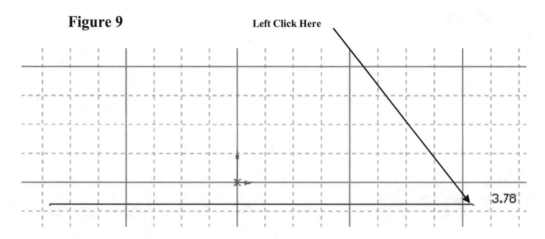

3.78

10

15.   While the line is still attached to the cursor, move the cursor towards the top of
       the screen and left click once. Notice the length of the line is attached to the
       cursor at the right as shown in Figure 10.

Figure 10   Left Click Once   Line Length

16. With the line still attached to the cursor, move the cursor towards the left side of the screen. Notice the line of small dots connecting the first and last point together. Left click once when the small dots appear as shown in Figure 11.

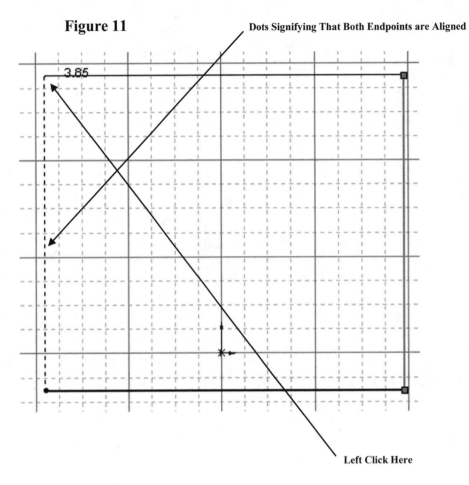

Figure 11

Dots Signifying That Both Endpoints are Aligned

3.85

Left Click Here

17. Your screen should look similar to Figure 12.

Figure 12

18. Move the cursor down towards the original starting point. Ensure that a red dot appears at the intersection of the two lines. This indicates that SolidWorks has "snapped" to the intersection of the lines. After the red dot appears, left click once. This will form a 90 degree box as shown in Figure 13.

Figure 13

Red Dot

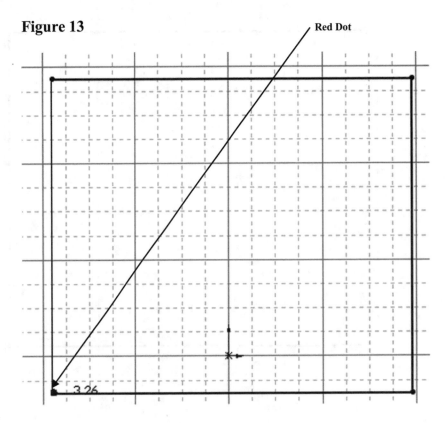

3.26

19. Your screen should look similar to Figure 14.

Figure 14

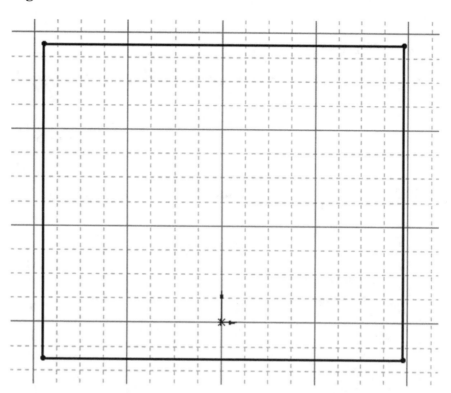

20. Move the cursor to the upper left portion of the screen and left click on the arrow to the right of SolidWorks. Left click on **Tools**. A drop down menu will appear. Left click on **Options** located at the bottom of the menu as shown in Figure 15.

Figure 15

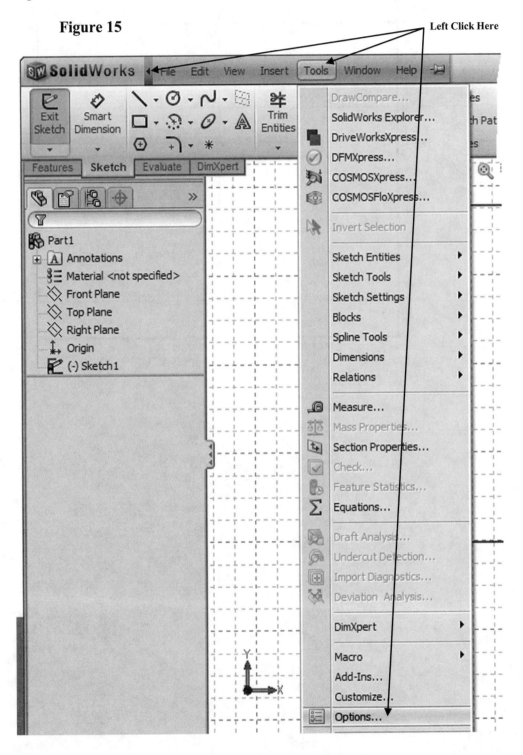

21. The Document Properties – Detailing dialog box will appear. Left click on the **Document Properties** tab. Left click on **Detailing**. Left click on the drop down arrow below the text "Dimensioning standard". A drop down menu will appear. Left click on **ANSI** as shown in Figure 16 (ANSI may already be selected).

Figure 16   Left Click Here   Left Click Here

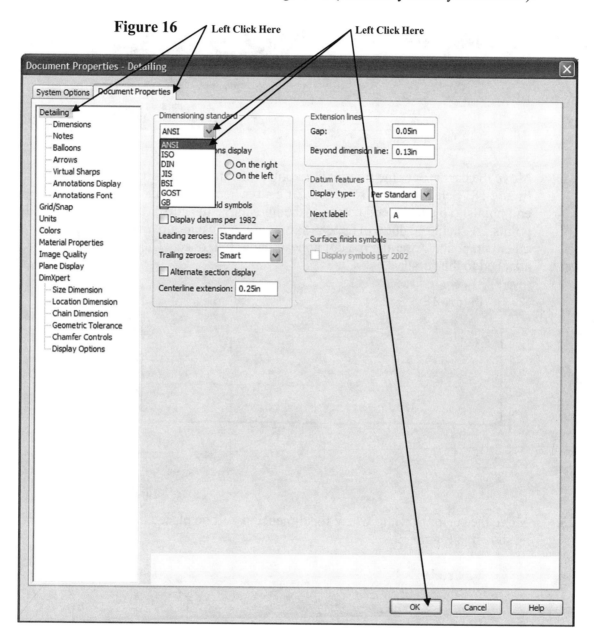

22. Left click on **OK**.

23. Move the cursor to the upper left portion of the screen and left click on **Smart Dimension** as shown in Figure 17.

Figure 17

Left Click Here

24. Move the cursor over the bottom horizontal line until it turns red as shown in Figure 18. Select the line by left clicking anywhere on the line **or** on each of the end points. To use the end points of the line, move the cursor over one of the end points. A small red dot will appear. Left click once and move the cursor to the other end point. After the red dot appears, left click once. The dimension will be attached to the cursor.

Figure 18

Turned Red

25. Move the cursor down to where the dimension will be placed and left click once as shown in Figure 19.

Figure 19

Left Click Here

4.55

26. The Modify dialog box will appear as shown in Figure 20.

Figure 20

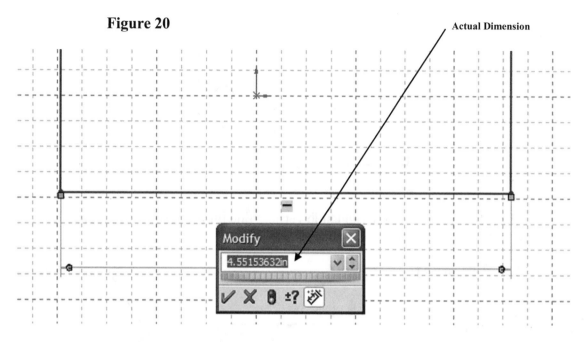

27. To edit the dimension, type **2.00** in the Modify dialog box (while the current dimension is highlighted) and left click on the green checkmark as shown in Figure 21.

Figure 21

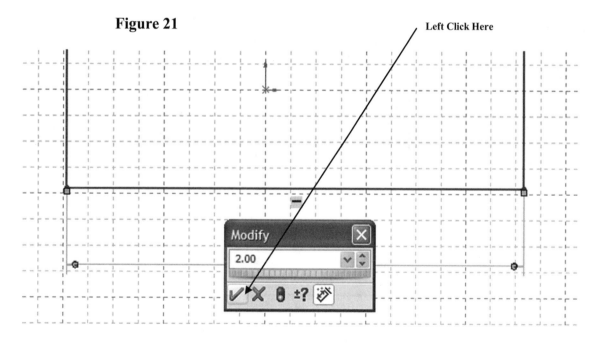

28.   The dimension of the line will become 2.00 inches as shown in Figure 22.

Figure 22

Dimension is Now 2.00

29.   Move the cursor over the right side vertical line until it turns red as shown in Figure 23. Left click once.

Figure 23

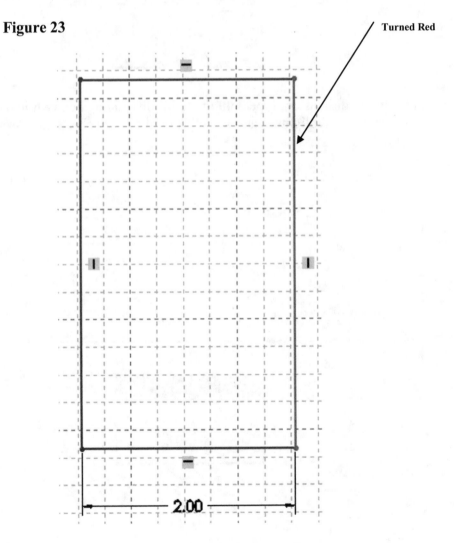

Turned Red

30.   Move the cursor to where the dimension will be placed and left click once as shown in Figure 24.

Figure 24   Left Click Here

31. The Modify dialog box will appear as shown in Figure 25.

Figure 25

32. To edit the dimension, type **.25** in the Modify dialog box (while the current dimension is highlighted) and left click on the green checkmark as shown in Figure 26.

Figure 26

33. The screen should look similar to Figure 27.

Figure 27

34. Right click anywhere around the drawing. A pop up menu will appear. Left click on **Select** as shown in Figure 28. This verifies that no commands are active.

Figure 28

Left Click Here

35. Move the cursor to the upper left corner of the screen and left click on **Line** as shown in Figure 29.

Figure 29

Left Click Here

36. Move the cursor to the upper left corner of the box as shown in Figure 30 and left
     click once.

Figure 30

37. Move the cursor upward to create a vertical line and left click once as shown in
     Figure 31.

Figure 31

38. Right click the mouse. A pop up menu will appear. Left click on **Select** as shown in Figure 32. This verifies that no commands are active.

Figure 32

39. You may have to zoom out to leave enough room to construct the following lines. To zoom out use the scroll wheel on the mouse or move the cursor to the upper middle portion of the screen and left click on the "Zoom to Fit" icon as shown in Figure 33.

Figure 33

40. Holding down the mouse wheel will allow you to rotate the sketch/part.

41. Move the cursor to the upper left corner of the screen and left click on **Line** as shown in Figure 34.

Figure 34

42.   Left click on the upper endpoint of the line. Move the cursor to the left and left click once as shown in Figure 35.

Figure 35

43.   With the line still attached to the cursor, move the cursor up and left click once as shown in Figure 36.

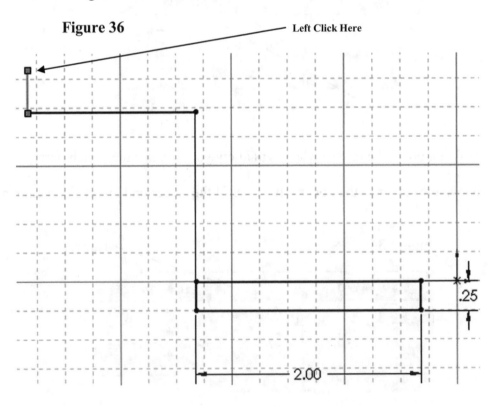

Figure 36

44. With the line still attached to the cursor, move the cursor to the right side of the screen and left click once as shown in Figure 37.

Figure 37

Left Click Here

.25

2.00

45. With the line still attached to the cursor, move the cursor down towards the bottom of the screen and left click once as shown in Figure 38. Notice the small green square appearing at the intersection of the two lines. After the left mouse button is clicked the green square will change to a green dot. This indicates that the lines are all connected.

Figure 38

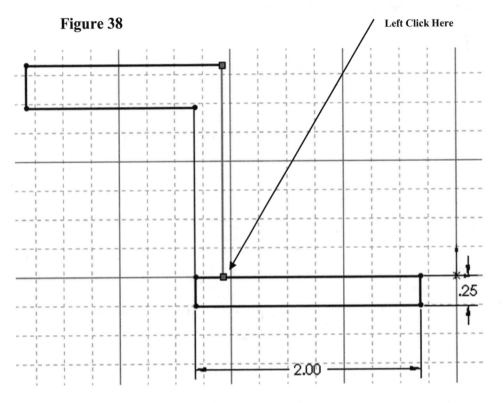

46. With the line still attached, right click the mouse. A pop up menu will appear. Left click on **Select** as shown in Figure 39. This verifies that no commands are active.

Figure 39

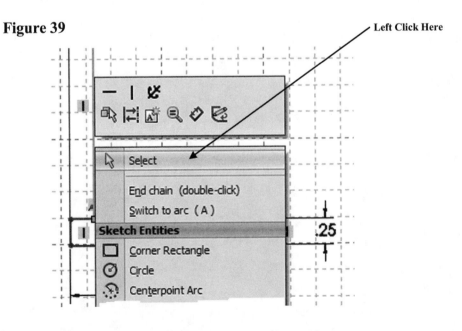

47. Move the cursor to the upper middle portion of the screen and left click on the the arrow below Trim Entities as shown in Figure 40.

Figure 40

48. More icons will appear. Left click on **Trim Entities** as shown in Figure 40.

49. Move the cursor over the line that will be trimmed and left click as shown in Figure 41. **NOTE:** After selecting **Trim Entities** move the cursor to the middle left portion of the screen and left click on **Trim to closest**. Now move the cursor over the line that will be trimmed and left click once.

Figure 41

50. The line will disappear as shown in Figure 42. Press the **ESC** key once. This verifies that no commands are active.

Figure 42

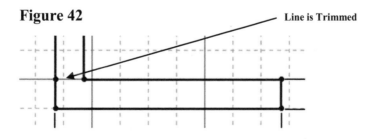

51. Move the cursor over the line in the lower left corner of the drawing as shown in Figure 43. The line will turn red. This particular line must be deleted so that the line above can be extended the full length.

Figure 43

Line To Be Deleted

52. Left click once on the line that will be deleted. The line will turn green with small green squares at each end as shown in Figure 44.

Figure 44

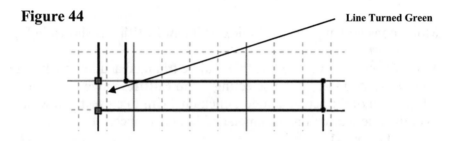

Line Turned Green

53. After the line is highlighted (turned green) right click once. A pop up menu will appear. Left click on **Delete** as shown in Figure 45.

Figure 45

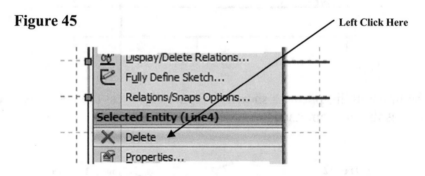

Left Click Here

54. The line will be deleted as shown in Figure 46.

Figure 46

Line is Deleted

55. Move the cursor to the upper middle portion of the screen and left click on **Trim Entities** as shown in Figure 47.

Figure 47

56. There are several different methods of trimming/extending a line.

57. Move the cursor over the line to be extended. It will turn red as shown in Figure 48.

Figure 48

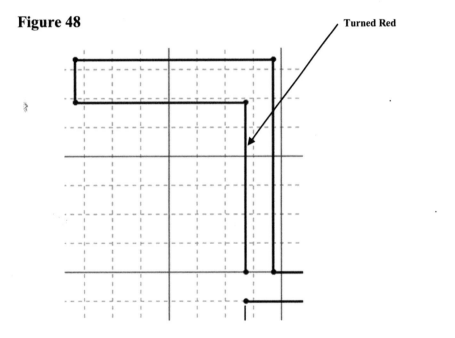

58. After the line has turned red, right click once. A pop up menu will appear. Left click on **Extend Entities** as shown in Figure 49.

Figure 49

59.   Move the cursor over the line to be extended. The line will extend downward forming one continuous line. Left click once as shown in Figure 50.

Figure 50

Left Click Here

60. Your screen should look similar to Figure 51.

Figure 51

61. Move the cursor to the upper left portion of the screen and left click on **Smart Dimension** as shown in Figure 52.

Figure 52

Left Click Here

33

62.   After selecting **Smart Dimension** move the cursor over the left side vertical line. The line will turn red as shown in Figure 53. Left click on the line.

Figure 53

63.   The dimension is attached to the cursor. Move the cursor to where the dimension will be placed and left click once. The Modify dialog box will appear as shown in Figure 54.

Figure 54

64. To edit the dimension, type **1.75** in the Modify dialog box (while the current dimension is highlighted) and left click on the green checkmark as shown in Figure 55.

Figure 55

65. The dimension is now 1.75 as shown in Figure 56.

Figure 56

66. Move the cursor over the left side vertical line until it turns red as shown in Figure 57. Left click on the line.

Figure 57

Turned Red

67. The dimension is attached to the cursor. Move the cursor back and forth to verify it is attached. Move the cursor to where the dimension will be placed and left click once. The Modify dialog box will appear as shown in Figure 58.

Figure 58

Actual Dimension

68. To edit the dimension, type **.25** in the Modify dialog box (while the current dimension is highlighted) and left click on the green checkmark as shown in Figure 59.

Figure 59

Left Click Here

69. The dimension is now .25 as shown in Figure 60.

Figure 60

70. Move the cursor over the top horizontal line until it turns red as shown in Figure 61. Left click on the line.

Figure 61

Turned Red

71. The dimension is attached to the cursor. Move the cursor up and down to verify it is attached. Move the cursor to where the dimension will be placed and left click once. The Modify dialog box will appear as shown in Figure 62.

Figure 62

Actual Dimension

72. To edit the dimension, type **1.75** in the Modify dialog box (while the current dimension is highlighted) and left click on the green checkmark as shown in Figure 63.

Figure 63

Left Click Here

73.   The dimension is now 1.75 as shown in Figure 64.

Figure 64

74.   Move the cursor over to the left side vertical line until it turns red and left click as shown in Figure 65.

Figure 65   **Left Click Here**

75.   Move the cursor to the other vertical line until it turns red and left click as shown in Figure 66.

Figure 66   **Left Click Here**

76. The dimension is attached to the cursor. Move the cursor back and forth to verify it is attached. Move the cursor to where the dimension will be placed and left click once. While the dimension is highlighted, left click the mouse once. The Modify dialog box will appear as shown in Figure 67.

Figure 67

77. To edit the dimension, type **.25** in the Modify dialog box (while the current dimension is highlighted) and left click on the green checkmark as shown in Figure 68.

Figure 68

78. Your screen should look similar to Figure 69.

Figure 69

79. Right click near the drawing. A pop up menu will appear. Left click on **Select** as shown in Figure 70. This will ensure that no commands are still active.

Figure 70

Left Click Here

80. Move the cursor to the upper left portion of the screen and left click on **Exit Sketch** as shown in Figure 71.

Figure 71

Left Click Here

81. Your screen should look similar to Figure 72.

Figure 72

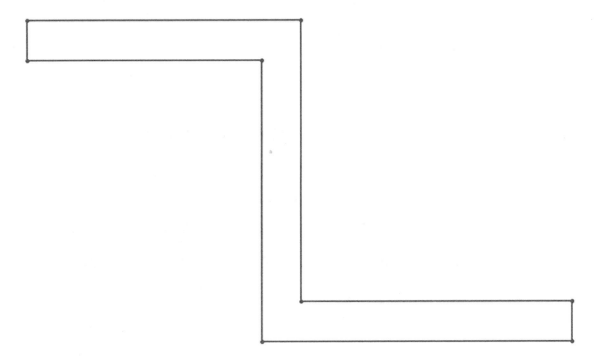

82.   To utilize the Features commands, a sketch must be present and have no opens (non-connected lines). If there are any opens in the sketch an error message will appear.

83.   Move the cursor to the upper middle portion of the screen and left click on the drop down arrow next to the "View Orientation" icon as shown in Figure 73.

Figure 73

84.   A drop down menu will appear. Left click on **Trimetric** as shown in Figure 74.

Figure 74

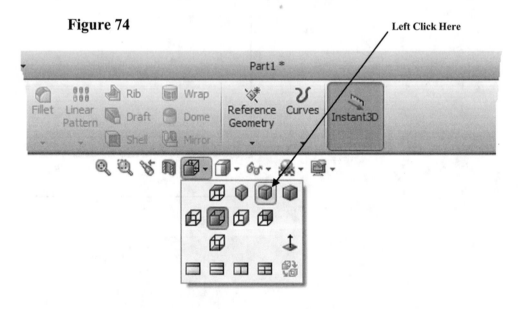

85. The view will become trimetric as shown in Figure 75.

Figure 75

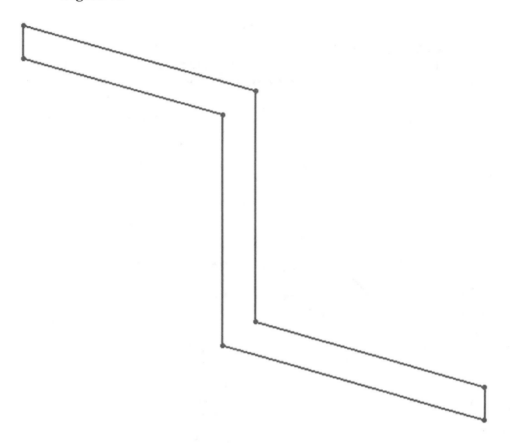

86. Move the cursor to the upper left portion of the screen and left click on **Extruded Boss/Base**. If the Extruded Boss/Base icon is not visible, left click on the **Features** tab as shown in Figure 76.

Figure 76   Left Click Here

87. The Extrude dialog box will appear. SolidWorks also provides a preview of the extrusion. If SolidWorks gave you an error message, there are opens (non-connected lines) somewhere on the sketch. Check each intersection for opens by using the Extend Entities and Trim Entities commands. Your screen should look similar to Figure 77. If the Extrude dialog box did not appear, left click on any line making up the sketch. To show shadows in the model left click on the drop down arrow to the right of the View Settings icon. A drop down menu will appear. Left click on **Shadows In Shaded Mode** as shown in Figure 77.

Figure 77

Left Click Here for Forward and Reverse Extrusion

Left Click Here if the Extrude Dialog Box did not Appear

Type 1.00 Here   Left Click Here to Turn on Shadows

88. Left click on the icon under Direction, located next to the text "Blind". The extrusion will change directions. Ensure that the extrusion is facing forward. While the text located next to "D1" is still highlighted, enter **1.000.** To preview the extruded part, left click on the "Glasses" icon located at the top of the Extrude dialog box as shown in Figure 78. The part will become purple.

Figure 78

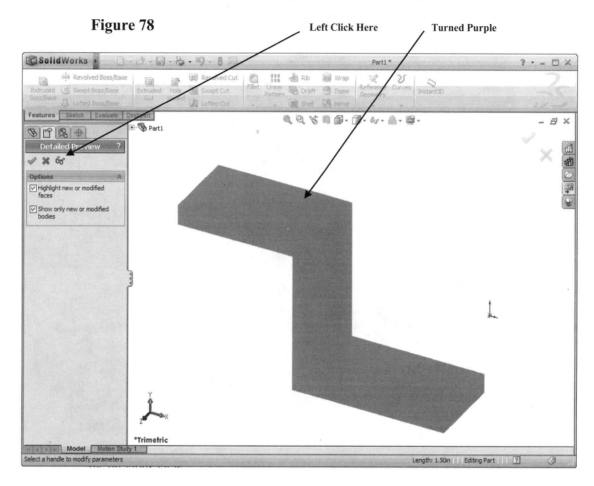

89. To end preview, left click on the "Glasses" icon again. This will return the part to the previous view.

90. Left click on the green checkmark as shown in Figure 79.

Figure 79

91.   Left clicking on the green checkmark will create a solid from the sketch. Your screen should look similar to Figure 80. Left click anywhere around the drawing.

Figure 80

92.   Move the cursor to the upper middle portion of the screen and left click on **Fillet** as shown in Figure 81.

Figure 81   Left Click Here

93. The menu at the left will change. Enter **.50** for the radius and select **Full Preview** as shown in Figure 82.

Figure 82

Enter .5 Here

Left Click Here To See Preview of Fillet

94.   Move the cursor over the lower front edge causing it to turn red and left click once as shown in Figure 83.

Figure 83

95.   Notice the yellow lines illustrating a preview of the fillet as shown in Figure 84.

Figure 84

96.   Move the cursor over the upper front edge causing it to turn red and left click once as shown in Figure 85.

Figure 85

97. Notice the yellow lines illustrating a preview of the fillet as shown in Figure 86.

Figure 86

Radius: 0.5in

98. Left click on the two upper remaining edges. You may have to use the rotate command to select the upper edge that is not visible.

99. Move the cursor to the upper middle portion of the screen and <u>Right</u> click on the drop down arrow to the right of the View Orientation icon. A drop down menu will appear. Place a check in the box (with the left mouse button) next to the "Rotate" icon as shown in Figure 87. The Rotate icon will now appear with the Viewing tools located at the top of the screen in the drawing area.

Figure 87

100. Left click on the left portion of the part (holding the left mouse button down). Drag the cursor to the right allowing access to the upper right corner of the part as shown in Figure 88.

Figure 88   Left Click Here, Hold Left Mouse Button Down, and Drag to the Right

Radius: 0.5in

101. Move the cursor to the upper middle portion of the screen and left click on the "Rotate" icon again if the backside of the part is not visible as shown in Figure 89. Once the part is in the desired position hit the **ESC** key to escape out of the Rotate command.

Figure 89   Left Click Here

102. Move the cursor to the upper right corners of the part causing the edges to turn red. Left click once as shown in Figure 90.

Figure 90

Left Click Here

103. Your screen should look similar to Figure 91.

Figure 91

104. Move the cursor to the upper right portion of the screen and left click on the drop down arrow next to the "View Orientation" icon as shown in Figure 92.

Figure 92

Left Click Here

105. A drop down menu will appear. Left click on **Trimetric** as shown in Figure 93.

Figure 93

106. Your screen should look similar to Figure 94.

Figure 94

107. Left click on the green checkmark as shown in Figure 95.

Figure 95

Left Click Here

108. Your screen should look similar to Figure 96.

Figure 96

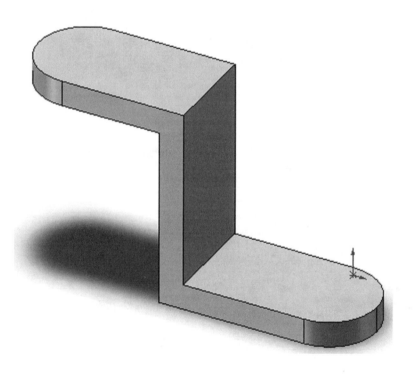

109. The next task will include cutting a hole in each of the ends. To do this, a sketch will need to be constructed on each surface. To begin a new sketch on any surface, move the cursor to the surface that will include the new sketch. Notice the edges of the surface are red. After the edges have turned red, right click on the surface as shown in Figure 97.

Figure 97

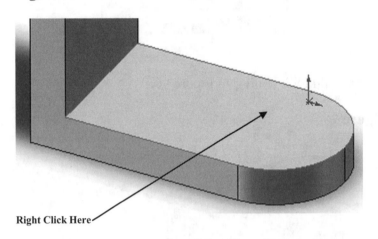

Right Click Here

110. The surface will change color. A pop up menu will appear. Left click on **Insert Sketch** as shown in Figure 98.

Figure 98

Left Click Here

Zoom/Pan/Rotate ▸

Recent Commands ▸

Face

3D Sketch On Plane

111. SolidWorks will create a "sketch" on that particular surface. Notice the toolbar at the top of the screen has changed back to the sketch commands.

112. Your screen should look similar to Figure 99.

Figure 99

113. Move the cursor to the upper left portion of the screen and left click on **Circle** as shown in Figure 100.

Figure 100   Left Click Here

114. Move the cursor to the edge of the circle. The center point of the circle will appear as shown in Figure 101.

Figure 101   Move Cursor Here

Center Point of Circle

115. After the center marker appears, left click on it once. This will be the center of a circle, which will later become a thru hole. Move the cursor out to the side to make the hole larger. Move the cursor out far enough to create a hole size similar to Figure 102.

Figure 102

116. After the hole size looks similar to Figure 102, left click once.

117. Move the cursor to the upper left portion of the screen and left click on **Smart Dimension** as shown in Figure 103.

Figure 103

118. Left click on the edge (not the center) of the circle as shown in Figure 104. The circle will turn red.

Figure 104

119. The dimension will appear attached to the cursor. Move the cursor up and down to verify it is attached. Move the cursor to where the dimension will be placed and left click once as shown in Figure 105.

Figure 105

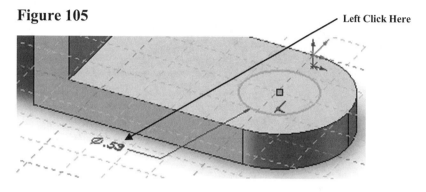

120. The Modify dialog box will appear as shown in Figure 106.

Figure 106

121. Type **.500** in the Modify dialog box and left click on the green checkmark as shown in Figure 107.

Figure 107

122. The diameter of the hole will become .500 inches as shown in Figure 108.

Figure 108

123. Right click near the drawing. A pop up menu will appear. Left click on **Select** as shown in Figure 109. This will ensure that no commands remain active.

Figure 109   Left Click Here

124. Move the cursor to the upper left portion of the screen and left click on **Exit Sketch** as shown in Figure 110.

Figure 110   Left Click Here

125. SolidWorks is now out of the Sketch commands and into the Features Commands. Notice that the commands at the top of the screen are now different. Also notice that the Features tab has is active as shown in Figure 111.

Figure 111

Features Tab

126. Move the cursor to the upper left portion of the screen and left click on **Extruded Cut** as shown in Figure 112. This time SolidWorks will extrude "space" or "air" rather than material as was done to create the bracket. If the command does not become active you will need to left click on the circle that was created in the sketch area.

Figure 112

Left Click Here

127. The menu at the left will change. Enter **.500** as shown in Figure 113.

Figure 113

Enter .500 Here

128. Move the cursor to the upper left portion of the screen and left click on the "Glasses" icon as shown in Figure 114.

Figure 114

Left Click Here

129. A preview of the part will be displayed as shown in Figure 115.

Figure 115

130. To return to the main menu, left click once on the "Glasses" icon.

131. Left click on the green checkmark as shown in Figure 116.

Figure 116

Left Click Here

132. There should be a thru hole in the part similar to Figure 117. Left click anywhere around the drawing

Figure 117

133. Another method of creating a hole is to use the Hole Wizard command.

134. To use the Hole Wizard command a "Point" must be constructed in the Sketch command. Move the cursor to the top portion of the part as shown in Figure 118. The outer edges of the part will turn red.

Figure 118

Move Cursor Here

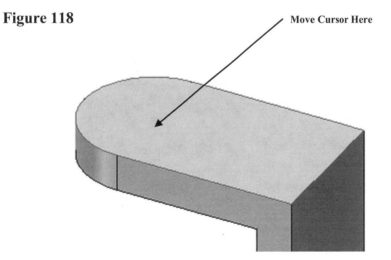

135. Right click on the surface. The surface will change color. A pop up menu will also appear. Left click on **Insert Sketch** as shown in Figure 119.

Figure 119

Left Click Here

136. SolidWorks will return to the Sketch commands as shown in Figure 120.

Figure 120

137. Move the cursor to the upper right portion of the screen and left click on **Point** as shown in Figure 121.

Figure 121

138. Move the cursor to edge of the part. A portion of the edge will turn red. The center point of the fillet radius will also appear. Left click once on the center point as shown in Figure 122.

Figure 122

139. A small center marker will appear on the center of the fillet radius as shown in Figure 123.

Figure 123

140. Move the cursor to the upper left portion of the screen and left click on the green checkmark as shown in Figure 124.

Figure 124

Left Click Here

141. Right click anywhere on the drawing. A pop up menu will appear. Left click on **Select** as shown in Figure 125.

Figure 125

Left Click Here

142. Right click anywhere on the drawing. A pop up menu will appear. Left click on **Exit Sketch** as shown in Figure 126.

Figure 126

Left Click Here

143. SolidWorks is now out of the Sketch commands and into the Features commands. Notice that the commands at the top of the screen are now different. Your screen should look similar to Figure 127.

Figure 127

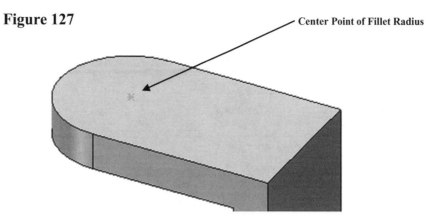

144. Move the cursor to the upper right portion of the screen and left click on **Hole Wizard** as shown in Figure 128.

Figure 128

145. The Hole Specification dialog box will appear. Left click on the Counter Bore icon. Place a check in the "Show custom sizing" box. Below Custom Sizing enter **.250** for Hole Fit and Diameter, **.500** for C'Bore Diameter and **.125** for the C'Bore Depth as shown in Figure 129.

Figure 129

Left Click Here

Enter .250 Here

Enter .125 Here   Enter .500 Here

146. Move the cursor to the top of the screen and left click on the **Positions** tab as shown in Figure 130.

Figure 130

Left Click Here

147. Move the cursor to the center point of the fillet radius and left click once as shown in Figure 131.

Figure 131

Left Click Here

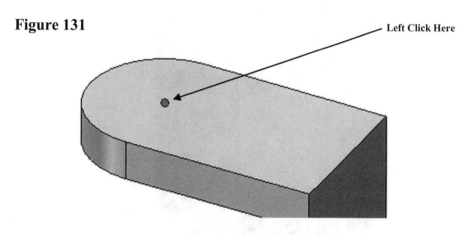

148. SolidWorks will provide a preview of the counterbore as shown in Figure 132.

Figure 132

149. Left click on the green checkmark as shown in Figure 133. Left click anywhere around the drawing.

Figure 133

150. Your screen should look similar to Figure 134.

Figure 134

151. To ensure that the hole is correct move the cursor to the top portion of the screen and left click on the "Rotate" icon as shown in Figure 135.

Figure 135

152. Left click anywhere around the part and hold the left mouse button down. Drag the cursor upward. The part will rotate upward as shown in Figure 136.

Figure 136

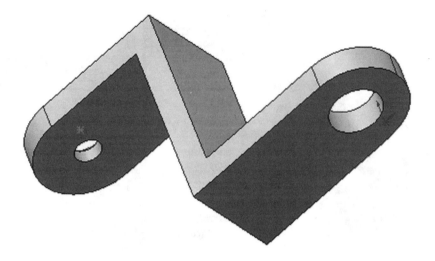

153. Holding the left mouse button down keeps the part attached to the cursor. To view the part in Trimetric, right click anywhere on the screen and left click on **View Orientation** as shown in Figure 137.

Figure 137

154. A drop down menu will appear. Double click on **Trimetric View** as shown in Figure 138.

Figure 138

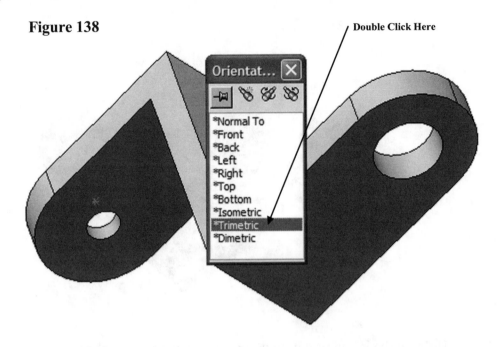

Double Click Here

155. Other commands for viewing are located at the top of the screen as shown in Figure 139.

Figure 139

Zoom To Fit   Standard Views

Zoom to Area (Window)   Previous View   Rotate

156.   The Zoom to Area (Window) command works by using the cursor to draw a window around the area you want to zoom in on. After selecting the "Zoom Window" icon, hold the left mouse button down and drag a diagonal box around the desired area. Release the left mouse button when the proper amount of zoom is achieved.

157.   The Zoom In/Out command works by scrolling the mouse wheel in either direction to achieve the desired view.

158.   The Pan command works similar to the Zoom In/Out command. Start by selecting the "Pan" icon. If the Pan icon is not visible with the other Viewing tools it will need to be added by using the same steps outlined on page 49. Once the icon has been added to the Viewing tools, left click on the icon. Left click on the drawing and hold the left mouse button down while moving the cursor up and down or side to side. Release the mouse button after the desired view is achieved.

159.   The Zoom to Fit command works by filling the screen so that the entire part is as large as possible while remaining visible in its entirety.

160.   The same viewing options can be accessed by right clicking anywhere on the drawing. A pop will be displayed as shown in Figure 140.

Figure 140

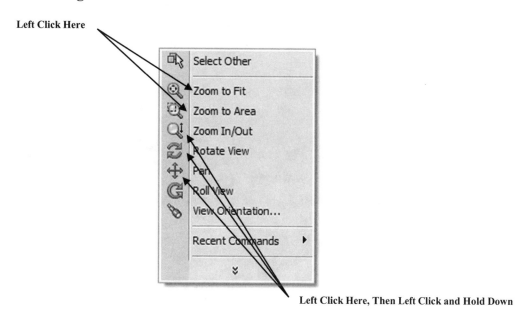

71

Drawing Activities

Problem 1

Problem 2

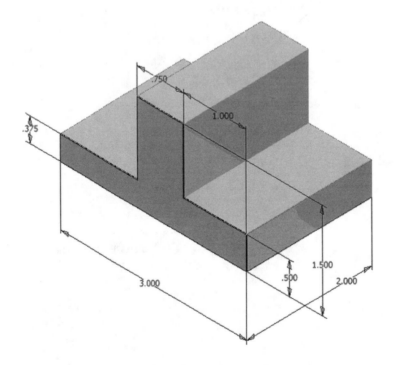

Problem 3

Extrude Center Section .25 Deep

Problem 4

Problem 5

Problem 6

Problem 7

Problem 8

Chapter 2 Learning More Basics

Objectives:
- Create a simple sketch using the Sketch commands
- Dimension a sketch using the Smart Dimension command
- Revolve a sketch using the Revolved Boss/Base command
- Create a hole using the Extruded Cut command
- Create a series of holes using the Circular Pattern command

Chapter 2 includes instruction on how to design the part shown below.

1. Start SolidWorks by referring to "Chapter 1 Getting Started".

2. After SolidWorks is running, begin a new sketch.

3. Move the cursor to the upper left corner of the screen and left click on **Line** as shown in Figure 1.

Figure 1

4. Move the cursor to the lower left portion of the screen and left click once. This will be the beginning end point of a line as shown in Figure 2.

Figure 2

5. Move the cursor to the right and left click once as shown in Figure 2.

6. Move the cursor up and left click once as shown in Figure 3.

Figure 3

7.   Move the cursor to the right and left click once as shown in Figure 4.

Figure 4

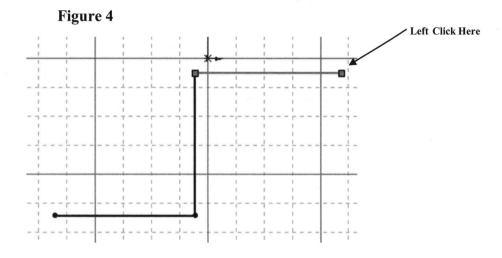

8.   Move the cursor up and left click once as shown in Figure 5.

Figure 5

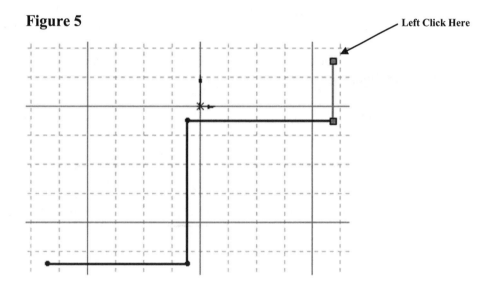

9. Move the cursor to the left. Ensure that the dots between the first end point and the last end point appear as shown in Figure 6. Left click once.

Figure 6

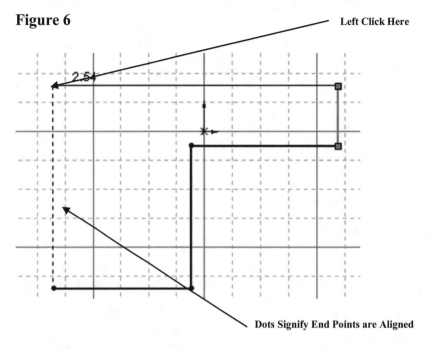

Left Click Here

Dots Signify End Points are Aligned

10. Move the cursor back to the original starting end point and left click once as shown in Figure 7.

Figure 7

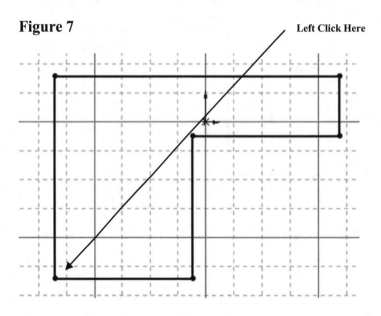

Left Click Here

11. Move the cursor to the middle left portion of the screen and left click on **Smart Dimension** as shown in Figure 8.

Figure 8

Left Click Here

12. After selecting **Smart Dimension** move the cursor over the bottom horizontal line until it turns red as shown in Figure 9. Select the line by left clicking anywhere on the line **or** on each of the end points. To use the end points of the line, move the cursor over one of the end points. A small red dot will appear. Left click once and move the cursor to the other end point. After the red dot appears, left click once. The dimension will be attached to the cursor.

Figure 9

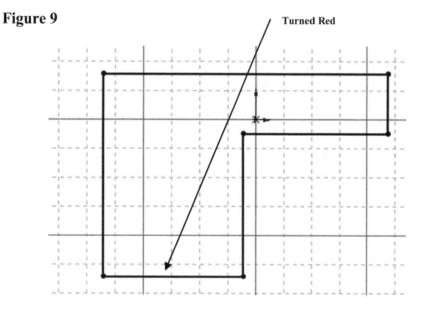

Turned Red

13.   Move the cursor to where the dimension will be placed and left click once as shown in Figure 10.

Figure 10

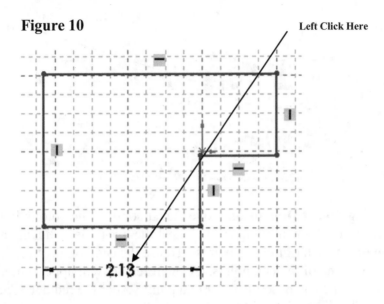

14.   The Modify dialog box will appear as shown in Figure 11.

Figure 11

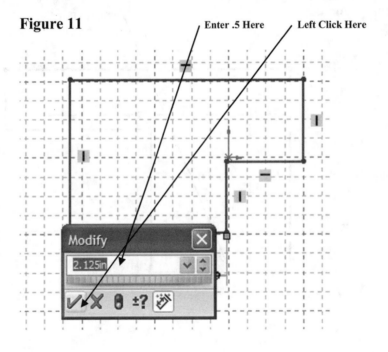

15. To edit the dimension, type **.5** in the Modify dialog box (while the current dimension is highlighted) and either press **Enter** on the keyboard or left click on the green checkmark as shown in Figure 11.

16. The dimension of the line will become .50 inches as shown in Figure 12.

Figure 12

17. To view the entire drawing move the cursor to the upper middle portion of the screen and left click once on the "Zoom To Fit" icon as shown in Figure 13.

Figure 13   Left Click Here

18. The drawing will "fill up" the entire screen. If the drawing is still too large, left click on the "Zoom In/Out" icon as shown in Figure 14. . If the Zoom In/Out icon is not visible with the other Viewing tools it will need to be added by using the same steps outlined on page 49. After selecting the icon, hold the left mouse button down and move the cursor up and down to achieve the desired view of the sketch.

Figure 14   Left Click Here

19.   Move the cursor to the middle left portion of the screen and left click on **Smart Dimension** as shown in Figure 15.

Figure 15   Left Click Here

20.   After selecting **Smart Dimension** move the cursor over the vertical line until it turns red as shown in Figure 16. Select the line by left clicking anywhere on the line **or** on each of the end points. To use the end points of the line, move the cursor over one of the end points. A small red dot will appear. Left click once and move the cursor to the other end point. After a red dot appears, left click once. The dimension will be attached to the cursor.

Figure 16   Turned Red

21. Move the cursor to where the dimension will be placed and left click once as shown in Figure 17.

Figure 17

Left Click Here

22. The Modify dialog box will appear as shown in Figure 18.

Figure 18

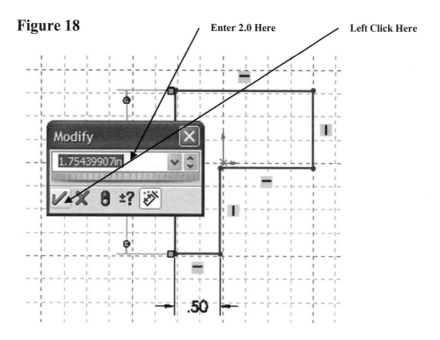

Enter 2.0 Here   Left Click Here

23. To edit the dimension, type **2.0** in the Modify dialog box (while the current dimension is highlighted) and either left click on the green checkmark (as shown in Figure 18) or press **Enter** on the keyboard.

24. The dimension of the line will become 2.0 inches as shown in Figure 19. Use the Zoom icons to zoom out if necessary.

Figure 19

25. Select the next line by left clicking anywhere on the line **or** on each of the end points. The dimension will be attached to the cursor.

Figure 20   **Line Turned Red**

86

26.   Move the cursor to where the dimension will be placed and left click once as shown in Figure 21.

Figure 21

Left Click Here

27.   The Modify dialog box will appear as shown in Figure 22.

Figure 22

Enter 1.5 Here   Left Click Here

28.   To edit the dimension, type **1.5** in the Modify dialog box (while the current dimension is highlighted) and either left click on the green checkmark (as shown in Figure 22) or press **Enter** on the keyboard.

29.   The dimension of the line will become **1.5** inches as shown in Figure 23. Use the Zoom icons to zoom out if necessary.

Figure 23

30.   Select the next line by left clicking anywhere on the line **or** on each of the end points. The line will turn red as shown in Figure 24. The dimension will be attached to the cursor.

Figure 24   **Turned Red**

31. Move the cursor to where the dimension will be placed and left click once as shown in Figure 25.

Figure 25

Left Click Here

32. The Modify dialog box will appear as shown in Figure 26.

Figure 26

Enter .75 Here   Left Click Here

33. To edit the dimension, type **.75** in the Modify dialog box (while the current dimension is highlighted) and either click on the green checkmark or press **Enter** on the keyboard.

34. The dimension of the line will become **.75** inches as shown in Figure 27. Use the Zoom icons to zoom out if necessary.

Figure 27

35. Move the cursor to the upper left corner of the screen and left click on **Line** as shown in Figure 28.

Figure 28
Left Click Here

36. Draw a line parallel to the top horizontal line as shown in Figure 29.

Figure 29
Draw This Line

37. Move the cursor to where the dimension will be placed and left click once. The Modify dialog box will appear. To edit the dimension, type **.25** in the Modify dialog box (while the current dimension is highlighted) and either click on the green checkmark or press **Enter** on the keyboard. Your screen should look similar to Figure 30.

Figure 30

Dimension Line .25 From Line Below

38. Right click anywhere on the drawing. A pop up menu will appear. Left click on **Select** as shown in Figure 31. This verifies that no commands are active.

Figure 31

Left Click Here

39. After the sketch is complete it is time to revolve the sketch into a solid.

40. Move the cursor to the upper left portion of the screen and left click on **Exit Sketch** as shown in Figure 32.

Figure 32

Left Click Here

41. SolidWorks is now out of the Sketch commands and into the Features commands. Notice that the commands at the top of the screen are now different. To work in the Features commands a sketch must be present and have no opens (non-connected lines). If there are any opens in the sketch an error message will appear. Your screen should look similar to Figure 33.

Figure 33

42. Move the cursor to the upper middle portion of the screen and left click on the drop down arrow next to the "View Orientation" icon. A drop down menu will appear as shown in Figure 34.

Figure 34

Left Click Here

43. Left click on **Trimetric** as shown in Figure 34.

44. The view will become trimetric as shown in Figure 35.

Figure 35

45. Move the cursor to the upper left portion of the screen and left click on **Revolved Boss/Base**. If the **Revolved Boss/Base** icon is not visible, left click on the **Features** tab as shown in Figure 36.

Figure 36

Left Click Here

46. If the box to the right of the axis symbol contains text, move the cursor to the "axis" line that was drawn above the part and left click once. The line will turn red. If the box to the right of the axis symbol does <u>not</u> contain text, left click inside the box, then left click on the axis line as shown in Figure 37. It may take several attempts to complete the revolve.

Figure 37

Left Click Here

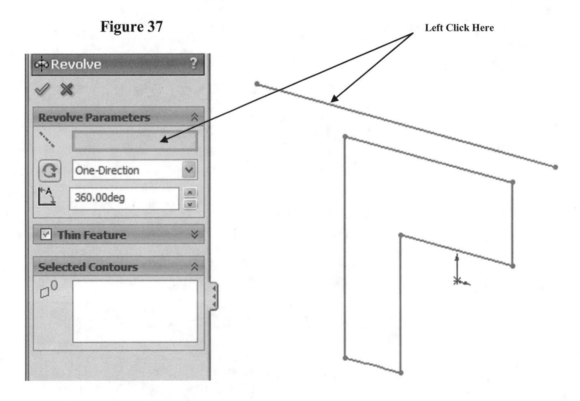

47. Move the cursor inside the profile causing it to turn red.

48. Move the cursor under "Selected Contours" and left click once. Left click inside the profile as shown in Figure 38.

Figure 38

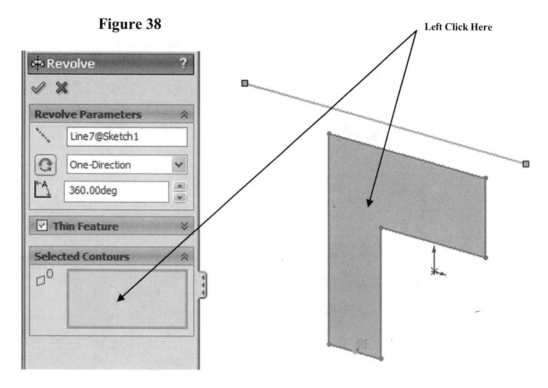

49. A preview of the revolve will appear as shown in Figure 39.

Figure 39

50.   Move the cursor to the middle left portion of the screen and left click on the checkmark next to the text "Thin Feature". <u>Remove the checkmark</u> (if needed) from the box as shown in Figure 40.

Figure 40

51.   Move the cursor to the upper left portion of the screen and left click on the green checkmark as shown in Figure 41.

Figure 41

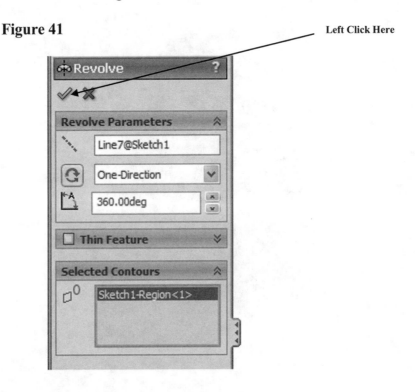

52. Your screen should look similar to Figure 42. You may have to use the zoom out command to view the entire part. Left click anywhere around the drawing.

Figure 42

53. Move the cursor to the edge of the part causing the edges to turn red. After the edges become red, right click on the surface as shown in Figure 43.

Figure 43

Right Click Here

54. The surface will turn green and a pop up menu will appear. Left click on **Insert Sketch** as shown in Figure 44.

Figure 44

Left Click Here

55. SolidWorks will begin a new sketch on the selected surface. Your screen should look similar to Figure 45.

Figure 45

56. Move the cursor to the upper right portion of the screen and left click on the drop down arrow next to the "View Orientation" icon. A drop down menu will appear. Left click on **Right** as shown in Figure 46.

Figure 46

57. SolidWorks will rotate the part to provide a perpendicular view of the selected surface as shown in Figure 47.

Figure 47

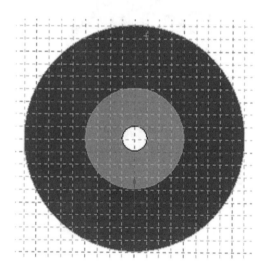

58. Move the cursor to the upper left corner of the screen and left click on **Line** as shown in Figure 48.

Figure 48

59.   Move the cursor over the small circle and wait a few seconds. A center marker
        will appear. Left click on the center marker as shown in Figure 49.

Figure 49

Left Click Here

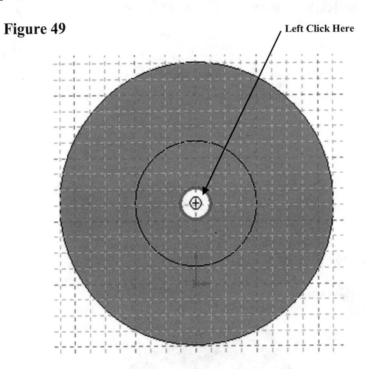

60. Move the cursor straight up and left click as shown in Figure 50.

Figure 50

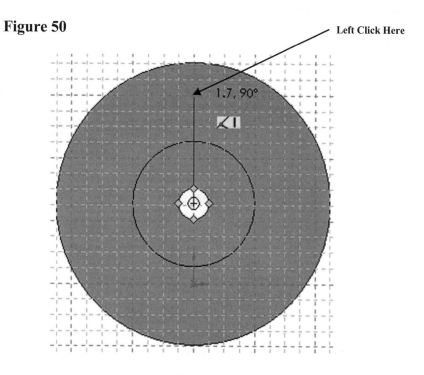

61. Now right click. A pop up menu will appear. Left click on **Select** as shown in Figure 51.

Figure 51

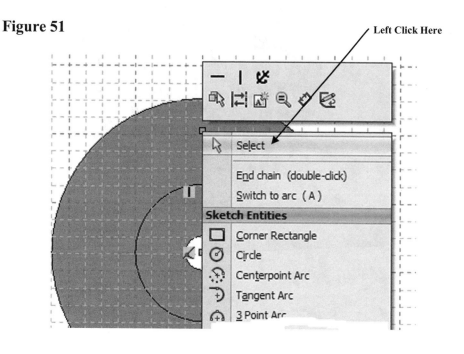

62. Move the cursor to the upper left portion of the screen and left click on **Smart Dimension** as shown in Figure 52.

Figure 52

Left Click Here

63. Move the cursor over the line that was just drawn. The line will turn red as shown in Figure 53. Select the line by left clicking anywhere on the line **or** on each of the end points. The dimension will be attached to the cursor.

Figure 53

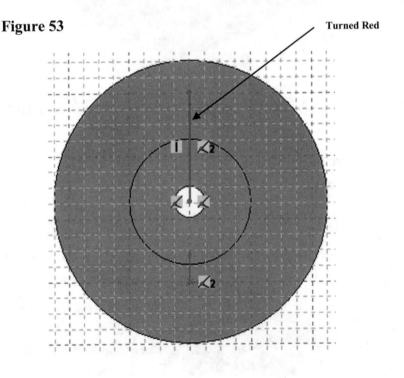

Turned Red

64. Move the cursor to where the dimension will be placed and left click once as shown in Figure 54.

Figure 54

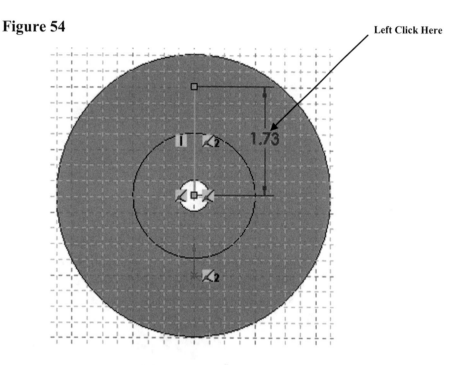

65. The Modify dialog box will appear as shown in Figure 55.

Figure 55

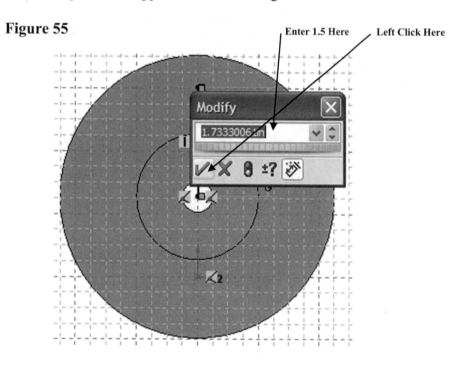

66. To edit the dimension, type **1.5** in the Modify dialog box (while the current dimension is highlighted) as shown in Figure 55. Left click on the green checkmark or press **Enter** on the keyboard.

67.   Right click anywhere on the screen. A pop up menu will appear. Left click on **Select** as shown in Figure 56.

Figure 56

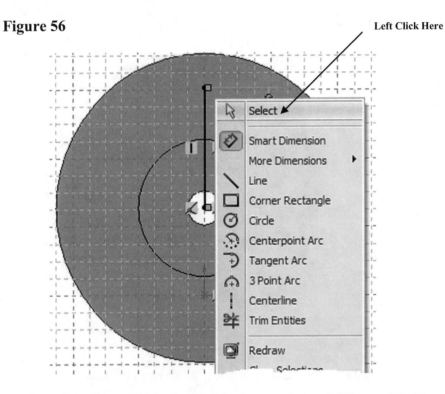

68.   The dimension of the line will become 1.5 inches as shown in Figure 55. Use the Zoom icons to zoom out if necessary.

Figure 57

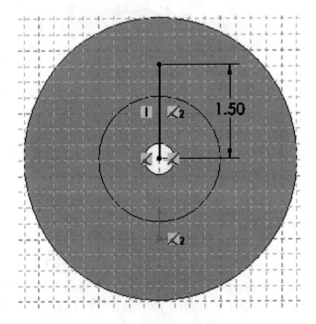

69. Move the cursor to the upper left portion of the screen and left click on **Circle** as shown in Figure 58.

Figure 58

Left Click Here

70. Left click on the endpoint of the line as shown in Figure 59.

Figure 59

Left Click Here

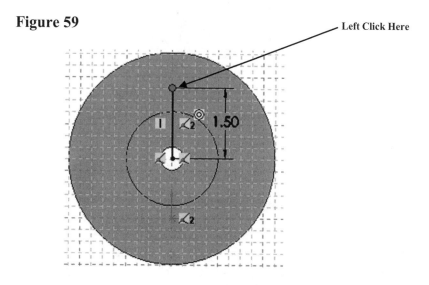

71. Move the cursor out to create a circle as shown in Figure 60.

Figure 60

Move Cursor Here

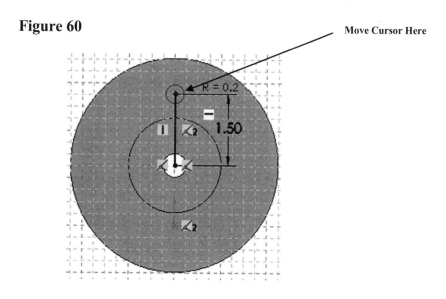

72. Left click as shown in Figure 61.

Figure 61

Left Click Here

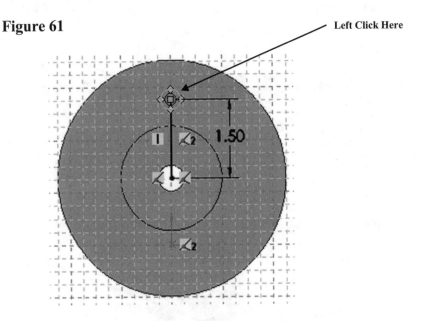

73. Move the cursor to the left portion of the screen and left click on the green checkmark as shown in Figure 62.

Figure 62

Left Click Here

74. Move the cursor to the middle left portion of the screen and left click on **Smart Dimension** as shown in Figure 63.

Figure 63

Left Click Here

75. Move the cursor to the circle that was just drawn. The circle will turn red. Select the circle by left clicking anywhere on the circle (not the center) as shown in Figure 64. The dimension will be attached to the cursor.

Figure 64

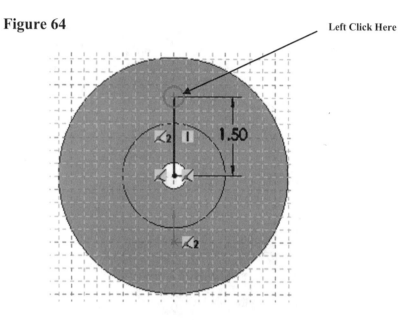

76. Move the cursor to where the dimension will be placed and left click once as shown in Figure 65.

Figure 65

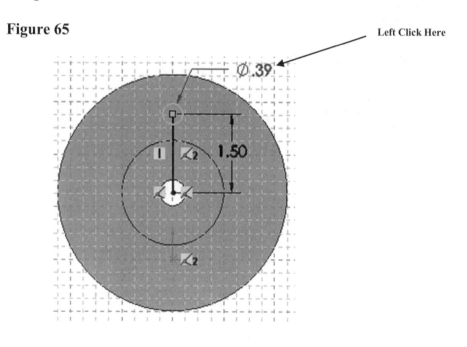

77. The Modify dialog box will appear as shown in Figure 66.

Figure 66

Enter 0.5 Here   Left Click Here

78. To edit the dimension, type **0.5** in the Modify dialog box (while the current dimension is highlighted) and either press **Enter** on the keyboard or left click on the green checkmark as shown in Figure 66.

79. The dimension of the line will become **0.5** inches as shown in Figure 67. Use the Zoom icons to zoom out if necessary.

Figure 67

80. Right click anywhere on the screen. A pop up menu will appear. Left click on **Select** as shown in Figure 68.

Figure 68

Left Click Here

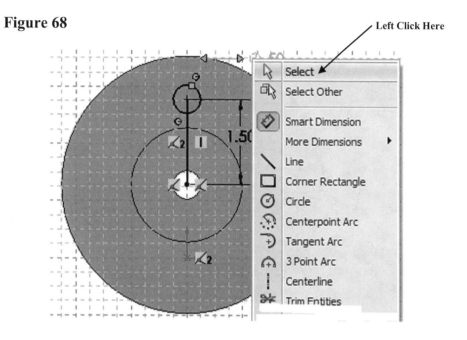

81. Move the cursor to the line that was used to locate the center of the circle. The line will turn red as shown in Figure 69.

Figure 69

Line Turned Red

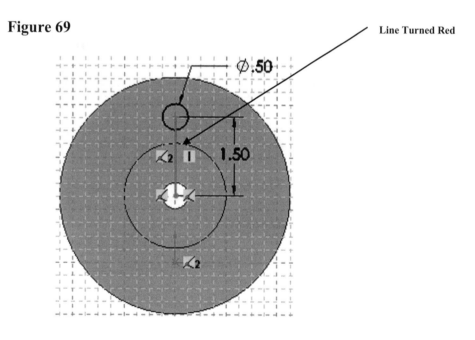

82.   Right click on the line after it turns red. A pop up menu will appear as shown in Figure 70.

Figure 70   **Left Click Here**

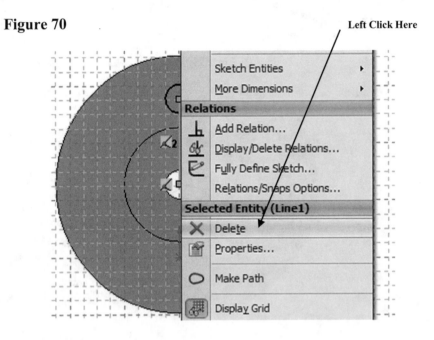

83.   Left click on **Delete** as shown in Figure 70.

84.   The Sketcher Confirm Delete dialog box will appear. Left click on **Yes** as shown in Figure 71.

Figure 71   **Left Click Here**

85. After you have verified that no commands are active, move the cursor to the upper left portion of the screen and left click on **Exit Sketch** as shown in Figure 72.

Figure 72

Left Click Here

86. SolidWorks is now out of the Sketch commands and into the Features commands. Notice that the commands at the top of the screen are now different. To work in the Features commands a sketch must be present and have no opens (non-connected lines). If there are any opens in the sketch an error message will appear. Your screen should look similar to Figure 73.

Figure 73

87. Move the cursor to the upper right portion of the screen and left click on the drop down arrow next to the "Views Orientation" icon. A drop down menu will appear. Left click on **Trimetric** as shown in Figure 74.

Figure 74

88. The view will become trimetric as shown in Figure 75.

Figure 75

89. Move the cursor to the upper middle portion of the screen and left click on **Extruded Cut.** If the **Extruded Cut** icon is not visible, left click on the **Features** tab as shown in Figure 76.

Figure 76   Left Click Here

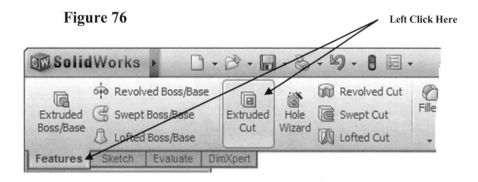

90. If SolidWorks did not provide a preview of the Extruded Cut, move the cursor to the edge of the circle. The edge will turn red as shown in Figure 77.

Figure 77   Turned Red

91. After the hole turns red, left click once.

92. A preview of the hole is displayed as shown in Figure 78.

Figure 78   **Arrow is Short and Depth of Hole is Shallow**

93. Move the cursor to the middle left portion of the screen. Highlight the text located next to D1 (as shown in Figure 79) and enter **.75** and press the enter key on the keyboard.

Figure 79   **Enter .75 Here**

94. Notice that the depth of the hole has changed in the preview. The arrow illustrating the hole depth is now longer as shown in Figure 80.

Figure 80

Longer Arrow Means Hole Depth is Deeper

95. Left click on the green checkmark as shown in Figure 81.

Figure 81

Left Click Here

96. Your screen should look similar to Figure 82.

Figure 82

Thru Hole

97. Move the cursor to the far right portion of the screen and left click on the arrows located below Reference Geometry as shown in Figure 83.

Figure 83

Left Click Here

98. A drop down menu will appear. Left click on **Axis** as shown in Figure 84.

Figure 84

Left Click Here

99. Move the cursor over the center of the center hole causing it to turn red as shown in Figure 85.

Figure 85

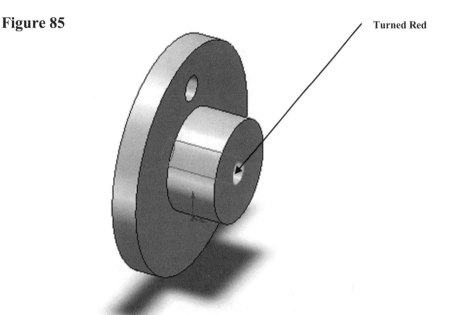

Turned Red

100. After the inside of the hole turns red, left click once. A center axis will be placed inside the hole as shown in Figure 86.

Figure 86

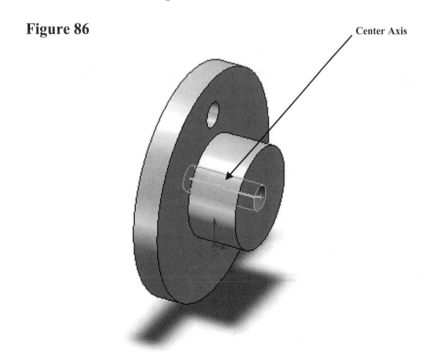

Center Axis

101. Move the cursor to the middle left portion of the screen and left click on the green checkmark as shown in Figure 87.

Figure 87

Left Click Here

102. Move the cursor to the upper middle portion of the screen and left click on the drop down arrow located below Linear Pattern. A drop down menu will appear. Left click on **Circular Pattern** as shown in Figure 88.

Figure 88

Left Click Here

103. Move the cursor to the inside edge of the hole. The outside edge of the entire hole will turn red. Left click once. Left click on the axis as shown in Figure 89.

Figure 89

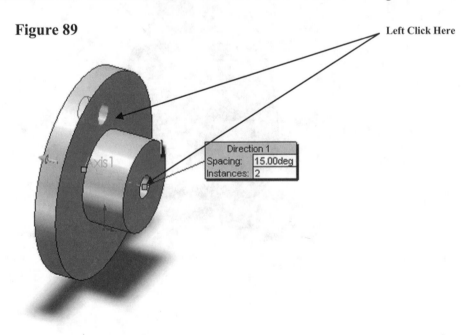

Left Click Here

104. Move the cursor to the left portion of the screen. Place a checkmark in the box next to the text "Equal Spacing". The degree amount automatically changes to 360 degrees. Enter **6** for the number of holes directly below 360 and press **Enter** on the keyboard as shown in Figure 90.

Figure 90

Enter 6 Here   Left Click Here

105. A preview of the circular pattern will be displayed as shown in Figure 91.

Figure 91

106. Move the cursor to the upper left portion of the screen and left click on the green checkmark as shown in Figure 92.

Figure 92   **Left Click Here**

107. Your screen should look similar to Figure 93.

Figure 93

108. To ensure that the holes are correct, move the cursor to the upper right portion of the screen and left click on the "Rotate" icon. If the Rotate icon is not visible move the cursor to the upper middle portion of the screen and <u>Right</u> click on the drop down arrow to the right of the View Orientation icon. A drop down menu will appear. Place a check in the box (with the left mouse button) next to the "Rotate" icon as shown in Figure 94. The Rotate icon will now appear with the Viewing tools located at the top of the screen in the drawing area. The Rotate command can also be made active by pressing the mouse wheel down and moving the cursor to achieve the desired view.

Figure 94

109. The part will rotate as shown in Figure 95.

Figure 95

110. Right click around the part. A pop up menu will appear. Left click on **Select**. Other viewing options are shown in the pop up menu in Figure 96.

Figure 96

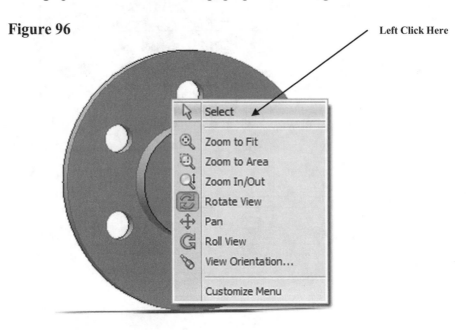

Left Click Here

Drawing Activities

Problem 1

Problem 2

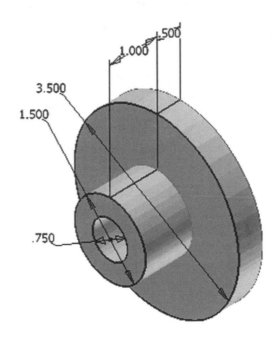

Problem 3

Revolve Axis

Problem 4

Revolve Axis

Problem 5

Problem 6

Problem 7

Problem 8

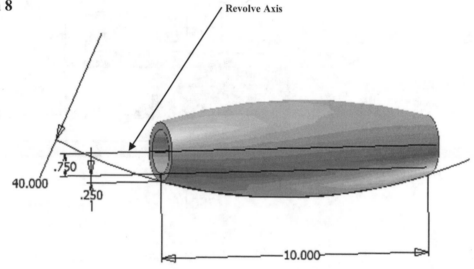

Chapter 3 Learning To Create a Detail Drawing

Objectives:

- Create a simple sketch using the Sketch commands
- Extrude a sketch into a solid using the Features commands
- Create an Orthographic view using the Drawing commands
- Create a Solid Model view using the Model View command

Chapter 3 includes instruction on how to design the parts shown below.

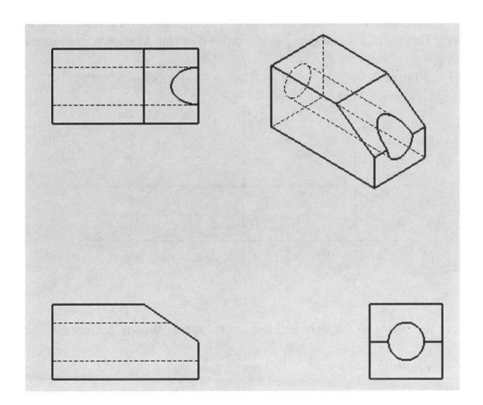

1. Start SolidWorks by referring to "Chapter 1 Getting Started".

2. After SolidWorks is running, begin a new sketch.

3. Move the cursor to the upper left corner of the screen and left click on **Line** as shown in Figure 1.

Figure 1

4. Move the cursor somewhere in the lower left portion of the screen and left click once. This will be the beginning end point of a line as shown in Figure 2.

Figure 2

5. Move the cursor to the right and left click once as shown in Figure 3.

Figure 3

6. Move the cursor upward and left click once as shown in Figure 4.

Figure 4

7. Move the cursor to the left and wait for dots to appear. Left click once as shown in Figure 5.

Figure 5

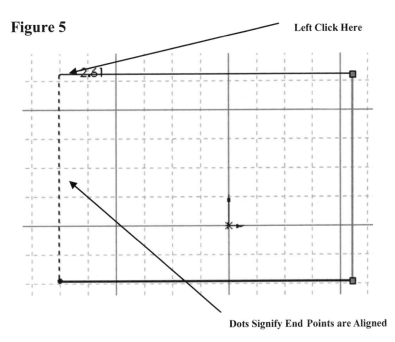

8. Move the cursor back to the original starting end point. A red dot will appear. Left click once. Your screen should look similar to Figure 6.

Figure 6   Left Click Here   Red Dot Signifies End Points are Aligned

9. Right click anywhere on the screen. A pop up menu will appear. Left click on **Select** as shown in Figure 7.

Figure 7   Left Click Here

10. Move the cursor to the upper middle portion of the screen and left click on **Smart Dimension** as shown in Figure 8.

Figure 8   Left Click Here

11. After selecting **Smart Dimension** move the cursor over the bottom horizontal line until it turns red as shown in Figure 9. Select the line by left clicking anywhere on the line **or** on each of the end points. The dimension will be attached to the cursor.

Figure 9

Turned Red

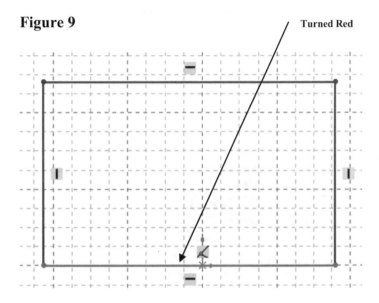

12. Move the cursor to where the dimension will be placed and left click once as shown in Figure 10.

Figure 10

Left Click Here

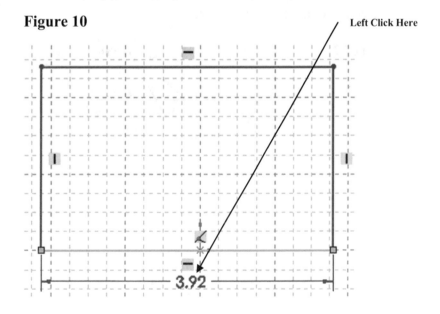

3.92

131

13.   The Modify dialog box will appear as shown in Figure 11.

Figure 11

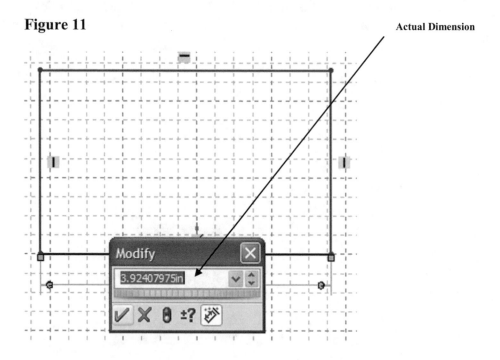

Actual Dimension

14.   To edit the dimension, type **2.00** in the Modify dialog box (while the current dimension is highlighted) and either press **Enter** on the keyboard or left click on the green checkmark as shown in Figure 12.

Figure 12

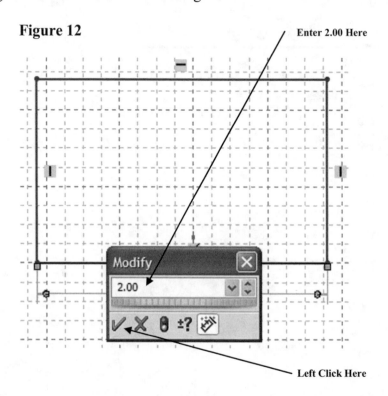

Enter 2.00 Here

Left Click Here

15. The dimension of the line will become 2.00 inches as shown in Figure 13.

Figure 13

16. Right click anywhere on the screen. A pop up menu will appear. Left click on **Select** as shown in Figure 14.

Figure 14   Left Click Here

17. To view the entire drawing, move the cursor to the upper right portion of the screen and left click once on the "Zoom to Fit" icon as shown in Figure 15.

Figure 15   Left Click Here

18. The drawing will "fill up" the entire screen. If the drawing is still too large, left click on the "Zoom In/Out" icon as shown in Figure 16. Hold the left mouse button down and move the cursor up and down to achieve the desired view of the sketch.

Figure 16   Left Click Here

19. Move the cursor to the upper left portion of the screen and left click on **Smart Dimension** as shown in Figure 17.

Figure 17   Left Click Once

20. Move the cursor over the right side line until it turns red as shown in Figure 18. Select the line by left clicking anywhere on the line **or** on each of the end points. The dimension will be attached to the cursor.

Figure 18   Turned Red

21. Move the cursor to where the dimension will be placed and left click once as shown in Figure 19.

Figure 19

Left Click Here

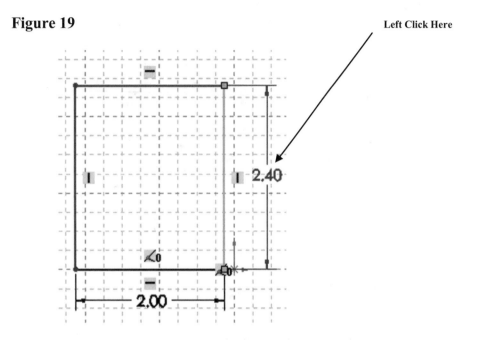

22. The Modify dialog box will appear as shown in Figure 20.

Figure 20

Actual Dimension

23.   To edit the dimension, type **1.00** in the Modify dialog box (while the current dimension is highlighted) and either press **Enter** on the keyboard or left click on the green checkmark as shown in Figure 21.

Figure 21

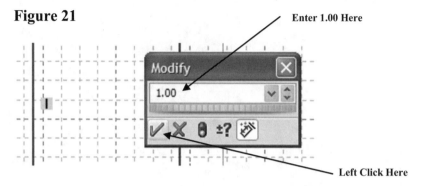

Enter 1.00 Here

Left Click Here

24.   The dimension of the line will become 1.00 inches as shown in Figure 22. Use the Zoom icons to zoom out if necessary.

Figure 22

25.   Right click anywhere on the screen. A pop up menu will appear. Left click on **Select** as shown in Figure 23.

Figure 23

Left Click Here

26. Move the cursor to the upper left portion of the screen and left click on **Smart Dimension** as shown in Figure 24.

Figure 24

Left Click Once

27. After selecting **Smart Dimension** move the cursor over the top horizontal line until it turns red as shown in Figure 25. Select the line by left clicking anywhere on the line **or** on each of the end points. This will cause the dimension to be attached to the cursor.

Figure 25

Line Turned Red

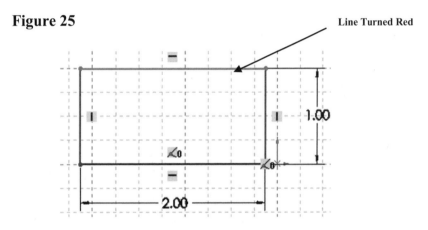

28. Move the cursor to where the dimension will be placed and left click once as shown in Figure 26.

Figure 26

Left Click Here

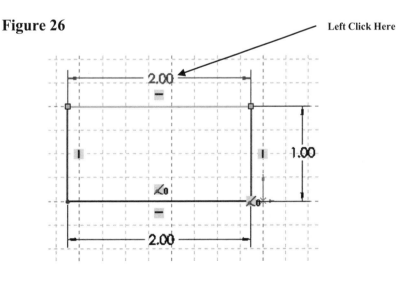

29. Notice that the dimension is exactly 2.000. Move the cursor to where the dimension will be placed and left click once. The Make Dimension Driven? dialog box will appear as shown in Figure 27.

Figure 27

Left Click Here

30. Right click anywhere on the screen. A pop up menu will appear. Left click on **Select** as shown in Figure 28.

Figure 28

Left Click Here

31. This dimension will over constrain the sketch because the sketch has been constrained with 90 degree angles when it was constructed. Left click on **OK**. The dimension will be driven meaning it cannot be used to edit or change the length of the line.

32. The driven dimension appears grayed out as shown in Figure 29.

Figure 29

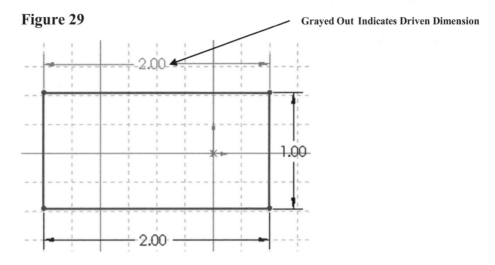

Grayed Out Indicates Driven Dimension

33. Dimensioning the far left line would also result in a driven dimension. Because of this, the dimensioning portion is complete.

34. After the sketch is complete it is time to extrude the sketch into a solid.

35. After you have verified that no commands are active, move the cursor to the upper left portion of the screen and left click on **Exit Sketch** as shown in Figure 30.

Figure 30

Left Click Here

36. SolidWorks is now out of the Sketch commands and into the Features commands. Notice that the commands at the top of the screen are now different. To work in the Features commands a sketch must be present and have no opens (non-connected lines). If there are any opens in the sketch an error message will appear. Your screen should look similar to Figure 31.

Figure 31

37. Move the cursor to the upper middle portion of the screen and left click on the drop down arrow next to the "Views Orientation " icon. A drop down menu will appear. Left click on **Trimetric** as shown in Figure 32.

Figure 32

38. The view will become trimetric as shown in Figure 33.

Figure 33

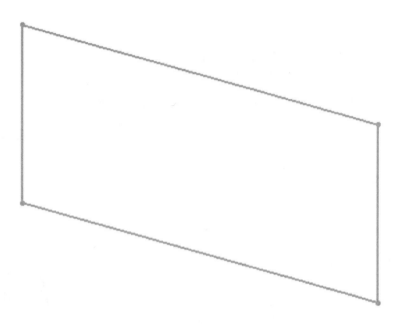

39. Move the cursor to the upper left portion of the screen and left click on **Extruded Boss/Base** as shown in Figure 34. If SolidWorks gave you an error message, there are opens (non-connected lines) somewhere on the sketch. Check each intersection for opens by using the **Extend** and **Trim** commands.

Figure 34

40. A preview of the extrusion will be displayed as shown in Figure 35.

Figure 35

41. If a preview does not appear, move the cursor over any of the lines. The line will turn red as shown in Figure 36. Left click once.

Figure 36   Turned Red

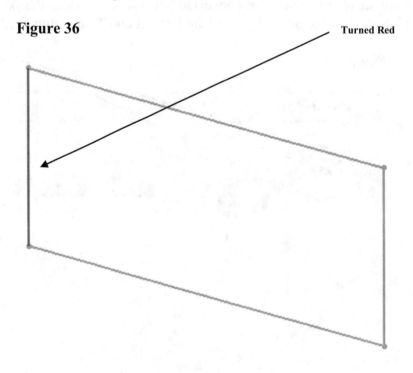

42.   Enter **1.00** for D1 as shown in Figure 37.

Figure 37

43.   Move the cursor to the upper left portion of the screen and left click on the green checkmark as shown in Figure 38. Left click once anywhere around the drawing.

Figure 38

44.   Your screen should look similar to Figure 39. You may have to use the Zoom Out command to view the entire part.

Figure 39

45.   Move the cursor to the upper middle portion of the screen and left click on the drop down arrow located under Fillet. A drop down menu will appear. Left click on **Chamfer** as shown in Figure 40.

Figure 40

46. After selecting **Chamfer,** place a dot (left click) next to the text "Distance distance". Place another dot (left click) next to the text "Full preview" as shown in Figure 41.

Figure 41

Left Click Here

47.   Move the cursor to the front upper corner. A red line will appear as shown in Figure 42. Left click once.

Figure 42

Line Turned Red

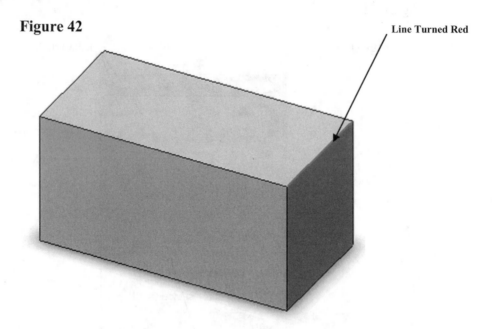

48.   A preview of the anticipated chamfer will be displayed as shown in Figure 43.

Figure 43

Anticipated Chamfer

Distance 1: 0.10in
Distance 2: 0.39370079in

49. Move the cursor to D1 in the Chamfer dialog box and highlight the text. Enter **.50.** Move the cursor to D2 in the dialog box and highlight the text. Enter **.75** as shown in Figure 44.

Figure 44

Enter .50 Here   Enter .75 Here

50. A preview of the chamfer will be displayed as shown in Figure 45.

Figure 45

Distance 1: 0.50in
Distance 2: 0.75in

51. Left click on the green checkmark as shown in Figure 46.

Figure 46

Left Click Here

Chamfer

52. Your screen should look similar to Figure 47.

Figure 47

53. Move the cursor to the upper middle portion of the screen and left click on the "Rotate" icon as shown in Figure 48.

Figure 48   **Left Click Here**

54. While holding the left mouse button down, drag the cursor to the right to gain access to the backside of the part as shown in Figure 49.

Figure 49

55. Right click anywhere on the screen. A pop menu will appear. Left click on **Select** as shown in Figure 50.

Figure 50

Left Click Here

56. Move the cursor to the upper middle portion of the screen and left click on the drop down arrow next to the "Views Orientation" icon. A drop down menu will appear. Left click on **Left** as shown in Figure 51.

Figure 51

Left Click Here

57. The part will rotate and provide a perpendicular view of the surface as shown in Figure 52.

Figure 52

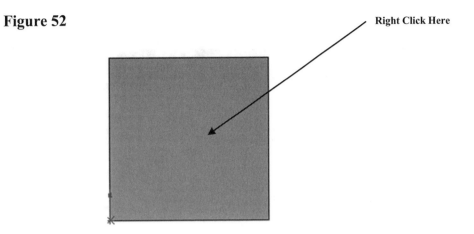

58. Right click anywhere on the surface. A pop up menu will appear. Left click on **Insert Sketch** as shown in Figure 53.

Figure 53

59. A new sketch will appear on the surface as shown in Figure 54.

Figure 54

60. Move the cursor to the upper left portion of the screen and left click on **Circle** as shown in Figure 55.

Figure 55   Left Click Here

61. Left click near the center of the part on the backside surface as shown in Figure 56.

Figure 56   Left Click Here

62. Move the cursor to the side forming a circle and left click as shown in Figure 57.

Figure 57

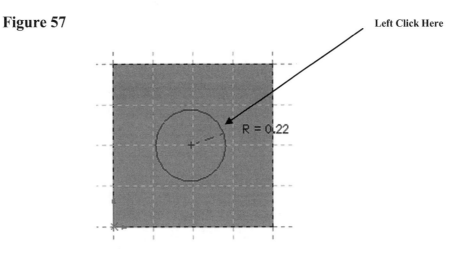

63. Right click anywhere on the screen. A pop up menu will appear. Left click on **Select** as shown in Figure 58.

Figure 58

64. Move the cursor to the upper left portion of the screen and left click on **Smart Dimension** as shown in Figure 59.

Figure 59

65.   After selecting **Smart Dimension** move the cursor over the edge of the circle
until it turns red as shown in Figure 60. Left click on the edge of the circle.

Figure 60   Turned Red

66.   Move the cursor to where the dimension will be placed and left click once as
shown in Figure 61.

Figure 61   Left Click Here

67. The Modify dialog box will appear as shown in Figure 62.

Figure 62

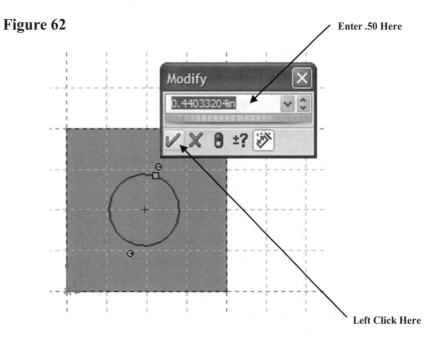

Enter .50 Here

Left Click Here

68. To edit the dimension, type **.50** in the Modify dialog box (while the current dimension is highlighted) and either press **Enter** on the keyboard or left click on the green checkmark as shown in Figure 62.

69. Your screen should look similar to Figure 63.

Figure 63

70. Move the cursor over the edge of the part until it turns red. Select the edge by left clicking anywhere on the edge as shown in Figure 64.

Figure 64

71. Move the cursor over the center of the circle until it turns red and left click as shown in Figure 65.

Figure 65

72. Move the cursor to where the dimension will be placed and left click once as shown in Figure 66.

Figure 66

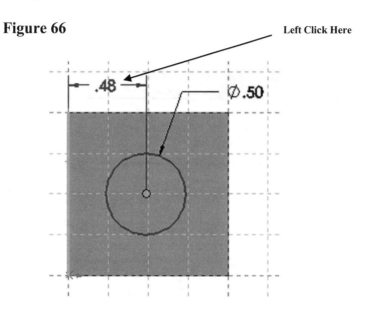

73. The Modify dialog box will appear as shown in Figure 67.

Figure 67

157

74. To edit the dimension, type **.500** in the Modify dialog box (while the current dimension is highlighted) and either press **Enter** on the keyboard or left click on the green checkmark as shown in Figure 68.

Figure 68   Left Click Here

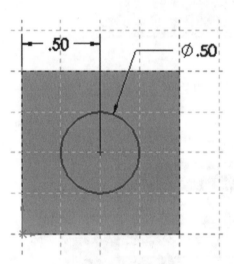

75. Your screen should look similar to Figure 69.

Figure 69

76. Move the cursor to the upper left portion of the screen and left click on **Smart Dimension** as shown in Figure 70.

Figure 70   Left Click Once

77. Move the cursor to the edge of the part until it turns red. Left click anywhere on the edge as shown in Figure 71.

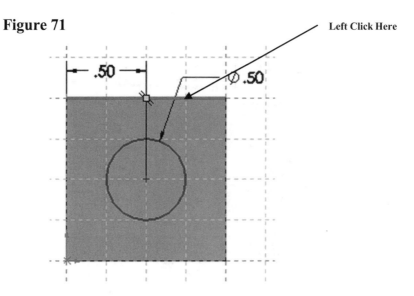

Figure 71

Left Click Here

78. Move the cursor over the center of the circle until it turns red and left click as shown in Figure 72.

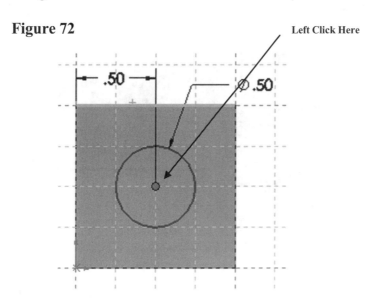

Figure 72

Left Click Here

79.   Move the cursor to where the dimension will be placed and left click once as shown in Figure 73.

Figure 73

80.   The Modify dialog box will appear as shown in Figure 74.

Figure 74

81.   To edit the dimension, type **.500** in the Modify dialog box (while the current dimension is highlighted) and either press **Enter** on the keyboard or left click on the green checkmark as shown in Figure 75.

Figure 75

82.   Your screen should look similar to Figure 76.

   Figure 76

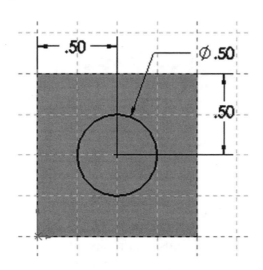

83.   After the sketch is complete it is time to extrude a hole through the solid.

84.   Right click anywhere on the screen. A pop up menu will appear. Left click on
       Select as shown in Figure 77. This will ensure that no commands are active.

   Figure 77

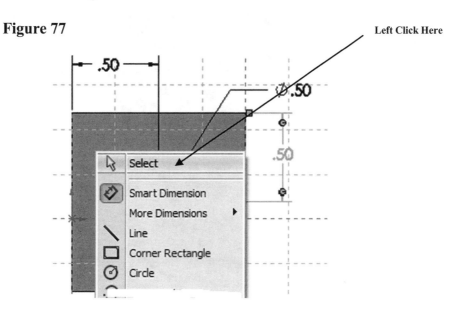

85.   After you have verified that no commands are active, move the cursor to the upper left portion of the screen and left click on **Exit Sketch** as shown in Figure 78.

Figure 78

Left Click Here

86.   SolidWorks is now out of the Sketch commands and into the Features commands. Notice that the commands at the top of the screen are now different. To work in the Features commands a sketch must be present and have no opens (non-connected lines). If there are any opens in the sketch an error message will appear. Your screen should look similar to Figure 79.

Figure 79

87.   Move the cursor to the upper middle portion of the screen and left click on the "Rotate" icon as shown in Figure 80.

Figure 80

Left Click Here

88. While holding the left mouse button down, drag the cursor to the right to gain an isometric view of the part as shown in Figure 81.

Figure 81

89. Right click anywhere on the screen. A pop up menu will appear. Left click on **Select** as shown in Figure 82.

Figure 82   Left Click Here

90. Move the cursor to the upper left portion of the screen and left click on **Extruded Cut** as shown in Figure 83. If you received an error message, there are opens (non-connected lines) somewhere on the sketch. Check each intersection for opens by using the **Extend** and **Trim** commands.

Figure 83

Left Click Here

91. Left click on the edge of the circle as shown in Figure 84.

Figure 84

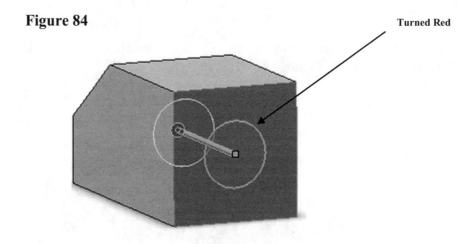

Turned Red

92. Enter **2.00** for D1 as shown in Figure 85.

Figure 85

Enter 2.00 Here

93. A preview will be displayed of the extrusion as shown in Figure 86.

Figure 86

94. Left click on the green checkmark as shown in Figure 87.

Figure 87

95. Move the cursor to the upper middle portion of the screen and left click on the drop down arrow next to the "Views Orientation" icon. A drop down menu will appear. Left click on **Trimetric** as shown in Figure 88.

Figure 88

96. Your screen should look similar to Figure 89.

Figure 89

97. Save the part file for easy retrieval to be used in the following section.

98. After the part file has been saved, move the cursor to the upper left portion of the screen and left click on the drop down arrow to the right of the "New Drawing" icon. A drop down menu will appear. Left click on **Make Drawing from Part/Assembly** as shown in Figure 90.

Figure 90

99. The Sheet Format/Size dialog box will open as shown in Figure 91.

Figure 91

100. Left click on **A-Landscape** as shown in Figure 91.

101. Left click on **OK**.

102. You can simply drag the any view, that you want to be the Front view, off of the View Palette at the right (not shown) on to the sheet. After placing the Front view move the cursor up and left click once. The Top view will be attached to the cursor and will appear. Continue placing the Side view and Isometric views. You may have to scale the views down after they have been dragged from the View Palette. Left click on the drop down arrow at the lower left portion of the screen under Use Custom Scale (not shown) and increase or decrease the scale factor. If the View Palette does not appear, move the cursor to the upper left portion of the screen and right click on **Sheet Format**. A pop up menu will appear. Left click on **Properties** as shown in Figure 92.

Figure 92

103. The Sheet Properties dialog box will appear. Left click next to Third Angle Projection. Left click on **OK** as shown in Figure 93.

Figure 93

104. The following tools should be visible. If the tools are not visible. Left lick on the **View Layout** tab as shown in Figure 94.

Figure 94

105. Move the cursor to the upper left portion of the screen and left click on **Standard 3 View** as shown in Figure 95.

Figure 95

106. If the file name you have been working on appears as shown in Figure 96, move the cursor over the file name and double click. If the file name does not appear, use the Browse button to locate the file. SolidWorks will create a 3 view drawing.

Figure 96

107. Move the cursor to the upper left portion of the screen and left click on **Projected View** as shown in Figure 97.

Figure 97

Left Click Here

108. Move the cursor to the Front View causing a red dashed box to appear. Left click inside the box as shown in Figure 98.

Figure 98

Left Click Here

109. Move the cursor to the upper right portion of the screen. An isometric view of the part will be attached to the cursor. Left click as shown in Figure 99.

Figure 99

Left Click Here

110. Move the cursor to the Front View causing a red dashed box to appear. Left click inside the box as shown in Figure 100. The Feature Manager will appear to the left.

Figure 100

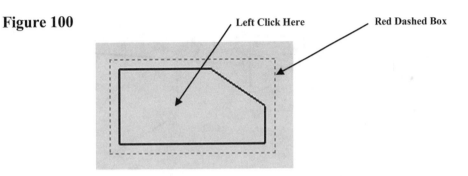

111. Move the cursor to the middle left portion of the screen under "Display Style" and left click on the "Hidden Lines Visible" icon as shown in Figure 101.

Figure 101

112. Move the cursor to the upper left portion of the screen and left click on the green checkmark as shown in Figure 102.

Figure 102

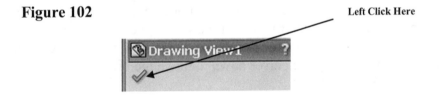

113. Your screen should look similar to Figure 103.

Figure 103

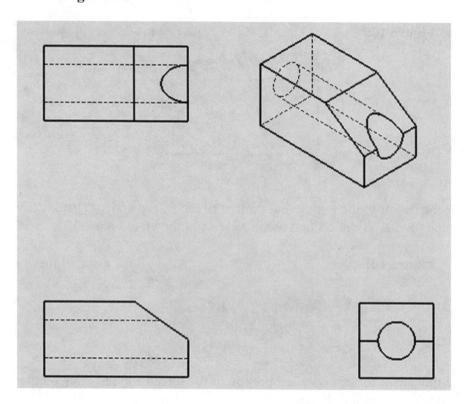

114. If for some reason the views need to be relocated, (moved closer together for example) move the cursor to any of the views (the top view in this case) causing red dots to appear and left click on the red dashed line (holding the left mouse button down). Drag the cursor down to move the view to the desired location as shown in Figure 104.

Figure 104

Left Click Here, Hold Down and Drag

115. Once the views have been moved closer together move the cursor to the upper left portion of the screen and left click on the green checkmark as shown in Figure 105.

Figure 105

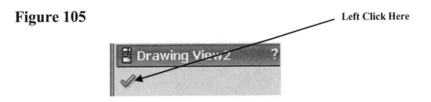

Left Click Here

116. Your screen may look similar to Figure 106.

Figure 106

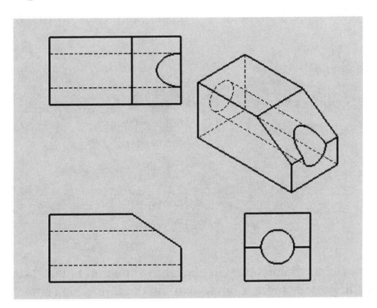

117. Move the cursor to the isometric view causing a red dashed box to appear around the part. Left click once. Move the cursor to the middle left portion of the screen and left click on the "Shaded with Edges" icon as shown in Figure 107.

Figure 107

Left Click Here

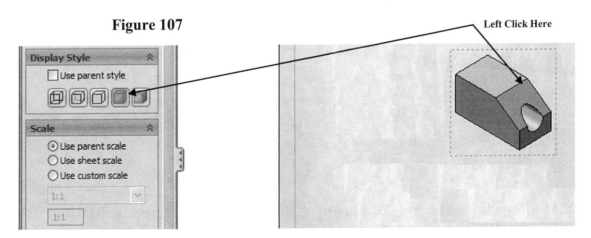

118.   Once you have created the isometric view, it will need to be deleted in order to create more room on the drawing. Move the cursor around the isometric view causing a red dashed box to appear around the part as shown in Figure 108.

Figure 108

Red Dashed Box

119.   Right click once. A pop up menu will appear. Left click on **Delete** as shown in Figure 109.

Figure 109

Left Click Here

120   The Confirm Delete dialog box will appear as shown in Figure 110. Left click on **Yes**. This will provide more room to work in the following chapter.

Figure 110

Left Click Here

121.   Save the part file as Part1.SLDDRW for easy retrieval. This part will be used in the following chapter. **Be sure to close SolidWorks completely out**.

Drawing Activities

Use these problems from Chapters 1 and 2 to create 3 view orthographic view detail drawings.

Problem 1

Problem 2

175

Problem 3

Problem 4

Problem 5

Problem 6

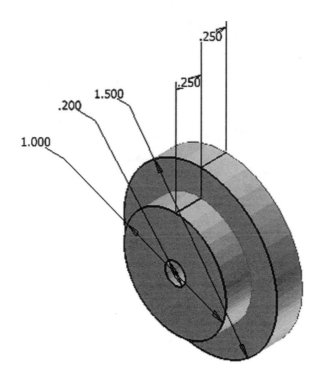

Problem 7

Revolve Axis

Problem 8

Revolve Axis

Chapter 4 Advanced Detail Drawing Procedures

Objectives:

- Create an Auxiliary View using the Auxiliary View command
- Dimension views using the Smart Dimension command
- Create a Section View using the Section View command
- Create Text using the Note command

Chapter 4 includes instruction on how to create the drawings shown below.

1. Start SolidWorks by referring to "Chapter 1 Getting Started". SolidWorks will have to be started up from "scratch" before you begin this chapter.

2. After SolidWorks is running, open the .SLDDRW file that was created in Chapter 3. Move the cursor to the upper left corner of the screen and left click on "Open" as shown in Figure 1.

Figure 1

3. The Open dialog box will appear. Left click on the drawing that was created in Chapter 3 as shown in Figure 2.

Figure 2

4. Left Click on **Open**.

5.   After the .SLDDRW file is open, move the views closer to each other to provide additional room on the drawing. Start by moving the cursor over the top view. Dots will appear around the view. Left click (holding the left mouse button down) on the dots and drag the view down closer to the front view as shown in Figure 3.

Figure 3   Left Click Here, Hold Down and Drag

6.   Move the side view closer to the front view.   Start by moving the cursor over the side view. Dots will appear around the view. Left click (holding the left mouse button down) on the dots and drag the view closer to the front view as shown in Figure 4.

Figure 4   Left Click Here, Hold Down and Drag

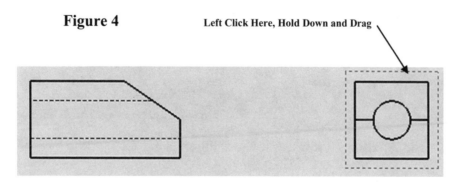

7. This will provide more room to work. Your screen should look similar to Figure 5. Press **ESC** on the keyboard.

Figure 5

8. Move the cursor to the upper left portion of the screen and left click on the **View Layout** tab as shown in Figure 6.

Figure 6

9. Notice that the commands at the top of the screen are now different as shown in Figure 7.

Figure 7

10. Left click on **Auxiliary View** as shown in Figure 8.

Figure 8

11.   Move the cursor to the wedge line and left click as shown in Figure 9.

Figure 9

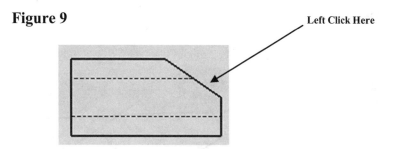

12.   SolidWorks will create an auxiliary view from the selected surface. The view will be attached to the cursor as shown in Figure 10.

Figure 10

13. Drag the cursor towards the other views and left click as shown in Figure 11.

Figure 11

Left Click Here

VIEW C-C
SCALE 1 : 1

14. Move the cursor over to the upper right portion of the screen and left click on the green checkmark as shown in Figure 12.

Figure 12

Left Click Here

Drawing View5

15. Your screen should look similar to Figure 13.

Figure 13

16. Move the cursor to the side view. Red dots will appear as shown in Figure 14.

Figure 14

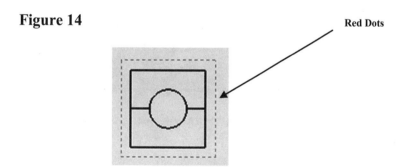

17.   Right click on the view. A pop up menu will appear. Left click on **Delete** as shown in Figure 15.

Figure 15

Left Click Here

18.   The Confirm Delete dialog box will appear. Left click on **Yes** as shown in Figure 16.

Figure 16

Left Click Here

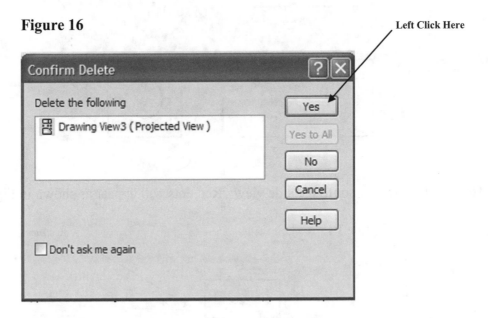

19.   Move the cursor to the upper middle portion of the screen and left click on **Section View** as shown in Figure 17.

Figure 17

Left Click Here

20.   Move the cursor over the front view. Red dots will appear around the view. Left click above the top of the part as shown in Figure 18.

Figure 18

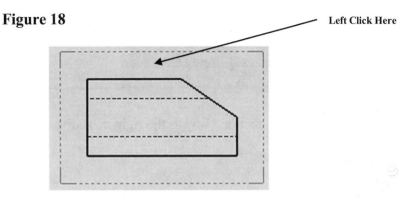

21.   Drag the cursor down across the part and left click as shown in Figure 19.

Figure 19

22.   Drag the cursor to the right. The section view will be attached to the cursor. Place a check in the "Flip Direction" box if cutting plane arrows are pointing the wrong direction. Place the section view to the side of the front view and left click as shown in Figure 20.

Figure 20

23. Move the cursor to the upper left portion of the screen and left click on the green checkmark as shown in Figure 21.

Figure 21

Left Click Here

24. SolidWorks will create a section view to the right as shown in Figure 22.

Figure 22

SECTION E-E
SCALE 1 : 1

25. Move the cursor to the upper left portion of the screen and left click on the **Annotation** tab as shown in Figure 23.

Figure 23

Left Click Here

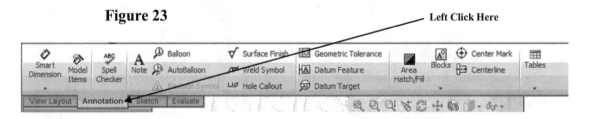

26. Notice that the commands at the top of the screen are now different as shown in Figure 24.

Figure 24

27. Annotations commands are typically where "drafting" activities are performed.

28. Move the cursor to the upper left portion of the screen and left click on **Smart Dimension** as shown in Figure 25.

Figure 25   Left Click Here

29. Move the cursor over the left side vertical line until it turns red as shown in Figure 26. Select the line by left clicking anywhere on the line **or** on each of the end points. To use the end points of the line, move the cursor over one of the end points. A small red dot will appear. Left click once and move the cursor to the other end point. After the red dot appears, left click once. The dimension will be attached to the cursor.

Figure 26   Left Click Here

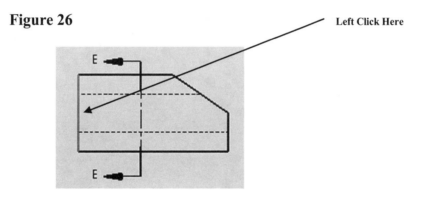

30. Move the cursor to where the dimension will be placed and left click once as shown in Figure 27.

Figure 27

31. Move the cursor to the upper left portion of the screen and left click on the green checkmark as shown in Figure 28.

Figure 28

32. Your screen should look similar to Figure 29.

Figure 29

33. Finish dimensioning the part to your own satisfaction. When the part is satisfactorily dimensioned, save the file to a location where it can be easily retrieved.

34. <u>If</u> there is ever a need to hide any dimension, move the cursor over the dimension. The dimension will turn red as shown in Figure 30.

Figure 30   Red Box

35. Right click on the dimension. A pop up menu will appear. Left click on **Hide** as shown in Figure 31. To retrieve the dimension, immediately left click on the **Undo** icon at the far upper middle portion of the screen.

Figure 31   Left Click Here

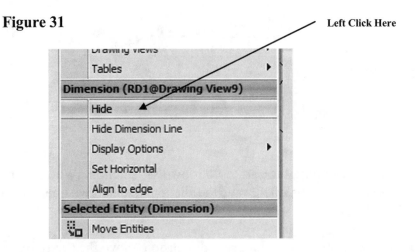

36. Left click on **Note** as shown in Figure 32.

Figure 32   Left Click Here

37.   Move the cursor to the title block location. A small box will be attached to the cursor. Left click as shown in Figure 33.

Figure 33

38.   The cursor will begin blinking. Enter your first name and last name. After the text has been entered, move the cursor to the upper left portion of the screen and left click on the green checkmark as shown in Figure 34.

Figure 34

39.   Text will appear in the title block as shown in Figure 35. Double clicking on the text will allow you to edit the text if needed.

Figure 35

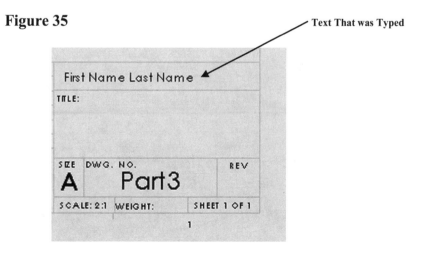

40. If the text needs to be moved, move the cursor over the text causing it to turn green as shown in Figure 36.

Figure 36

Left Click and Drag Here

First Name Last Name

41. While the text is green, left click (holding the left mouse button down) and drag the text to the desired location. After the text is in the desired location, release the left mouse button.

42. Your screen should look similar to Figure 37.

Figure 37

43.   Save the current sheet where it can be easily retrieved.

Drawing Activities

Create Section View Drawings for the following:

Problem 1

Problem 2

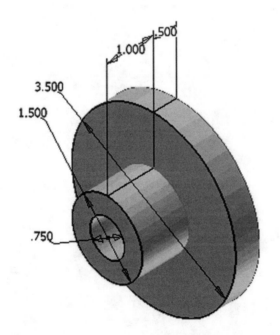

Create Auxiliary View Drawings for the following:

Problem 3

Extrude Center Section .25 Deep

Problem 4

Create Section View Drawings for the following:

Problem 5

Problem 6

Create Section View Drawings for the following:

Problem 7

Problem 8

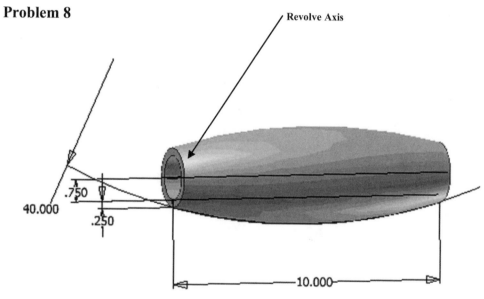

Chapter 5 Learning To Edit Existing Solid Models

Objectives:

- Design a simple part
- Learn to use the Circular Pattern command
- Learn to edit a part using the Circular Pattern command
- Edit the part using the Sketch command
- Edit the part using the Extruded Boss/Base command
- Edit the part using the Extruded Cut command
- Edit the part using the Chamfer command

Chapter 5 includes instruction on how to design and edit the part shown below.

1.   Start SolidWorks by referring to "Chapter 1 Getting Started".

2.   After SolidWorks is running, begin a new sketch.

3.   Move the cursor to the upper left corner of the screen and left click on **Circle** as shown in Figure 1.

Figure 1

4.   Move the cursor to the center of the screen and left click once. This will be the center of the circle as shown in Figure 2.

Figure 2

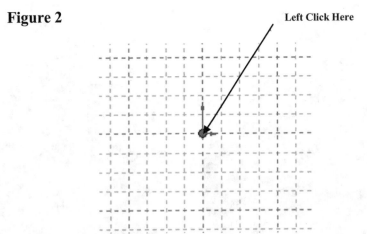

5.   Move the cursor to the right and left click once as shown in Figure 3.

Figure 3

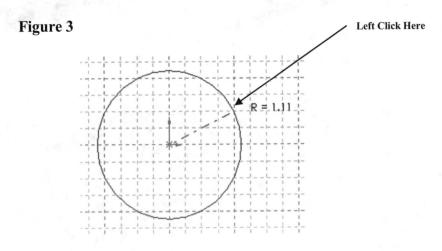

6. Right click anywhere on the drawing. A pop up menu will appear. Left click on **Select** as shown in Figure 4

Figure 4

7. Move the cursor to the middle left portion of the screen and left click on **Smart Dimension** as shown in Figure 5.

Figure 5

8. Move the cursor over the edge (not center) of the circle until it turns red. Left click once as shown in Figure 6. The dimension will be attached to the cursor.

Figure 6

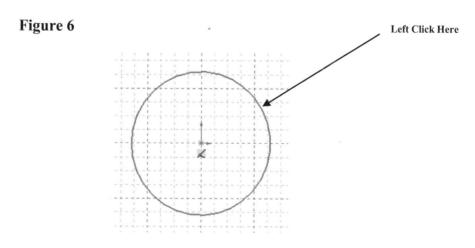

9.   Move the cursor to where the dimension will be placed and left click once as shown in Figure 7.

Figure 7

Enter 2.000 Here

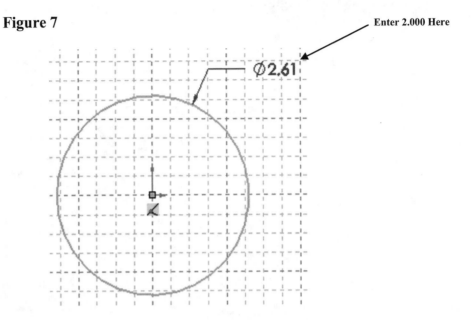

10.   The Modify dialog box will appear as shown in Figure 8.

Figure 8

Enter 2.00 Here

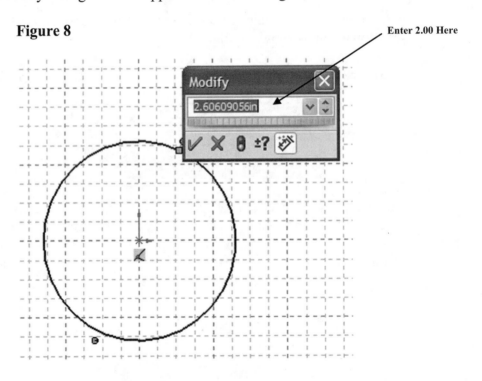

11. To edit the dimension, type **2.00** in the Modify dialog box (while the current dimension is highlighted) and left click on the green checkmark as shown in Figure 9.

Figure 9

Left Click Here

12. The dimension of the circle will become 2.00 inches as shown in Figure 10.

Figure 10

Left Click Here

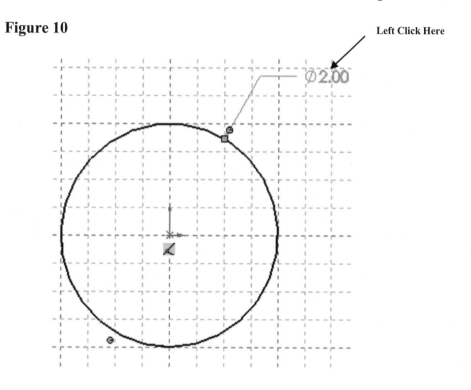

13. Right click anywhere around the drawing. A pop up menu will appear. Left click on **Select** as shown in Figure 11.

Figure 11

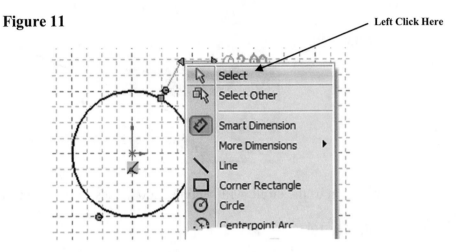

14. To view the entire drawing move the cursor to the middle portion of the screen and left click on the "Zoom To Fit" icon as shown in Figure 12.

Figure 12

15. The drawing will "fill up" the entire screen. If the drawing is still too large, left click on the "Zoom In/Out" icon as shown in Figure 13. After selecting the "Zoom In/Out icon, hold the left mouse button down and drag the cursor up and down to achieve the desired view of the sketch.

Figure 13

206

16. After the sketch is complete it is time to extrude the sketch into a solid. Right click anywhere on the drawing. A pop up menu will appear. Left click on **Select** as shown in Figure 14.

Figure 14

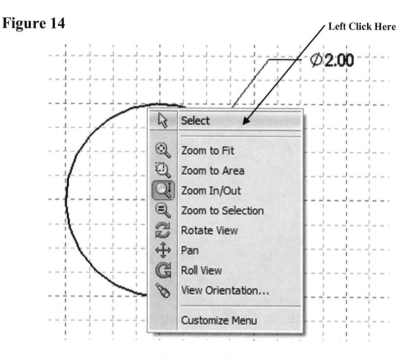

17. After you have verified that no commands are active, right click anywhere on the sketch. A pop up menu will appear. Left click on the **Exit Sketch** icon as shown in Figure 15. If the Features tools did not appear, left click on the **Features** tab at the upper left portion of the screen.

Figure 15

18.   SolidWorks is now out of the Sketch commands and into the Features commands. Notice that the commands at the top of the screen and now different. To work in the Features commands a sketch must be present and have no opens (non-connected lines). If there are any opens in the sketch an error message will appear. You screen should look similar to Figure 16.

Figure 16

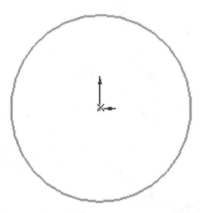

19.   Move the cursor to the upper middle portion of the screen and left click on the drop down arrow next to the "Views Orientation" icon. A drop down menu will appear. Left click on **Trimetric** as shown in Figure 17.

Figure 17

Left Click Here

20. The view will become trimetric as shown in Figure 18.

Figure 18

21. Move the cursor to the upper left portion of the screen and left click on **Extruded Boss/Bass** as shown in Figure 19.

Figure 19   Left Click Here

22. A preview of the extrusion will be displayed. <u>If a preview is not displayed, left click anywhere on the edge of the circle.</u> If SolidWorks gave you an error message, there are opens (non-connected lines) somewhere on the sketch. Check each intersection for opens by using the **Extend** and **Trim** commands.

23. Move the cursor to the upper left portion of the screen and enter **.25** next to D1 as shown in Figure 20.

Figure 20

Enter .25 Here

24. Move the cursor to the upper left portion of the screen and left click on the green checkmark as shown in Figure 21.

Figure 21

Left Click Here

25. Your screen should look similar to Figure 22.

Figure 22

26. Move the cursor to the front surface causing the edges of the surface to turn red. Right click on the surface once. A pop up menu will appear. Left click on the **Insert Sketch** icon as shown in Figure 23.

Figure 23   Left Click Here

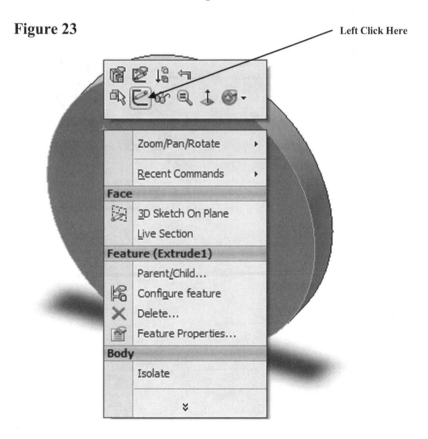

27.   SolidWorks will start a new sketch on the selected surface as shown in Figure 24.

Figure 24

Left Click Here

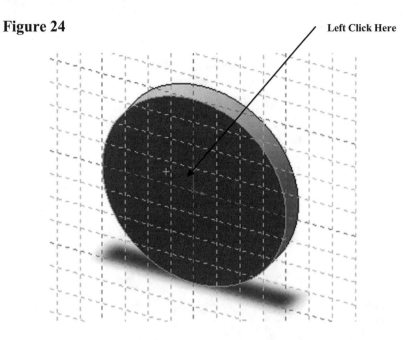

28.   Move the cursor to the upper right portion of the screen and left click on the drop down arrow next to the "Standard Views" icon. A drop down menu will appear. Left click on the **Front** icon. You can also left click on the **Normal To** icon as shown in Figure 25.

Figure 25

Left Click Here

29. The part will rotate providing a perpendicular view of the surface as shown in Figure 26.

Figure 26

30. Move the cursor to the upper middle portion of the screen and left click on **Circle** as shown in Figure 27.

Figure 27

31. Move the cursor to the center of the circle. A red dot will appear in the center as shown in Figure 28.

Figure 28

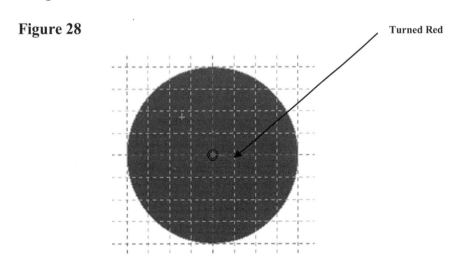

32.   After the red dot appears, move the cursor straight up causing a blue dashed line to appear. Left click once as shown in Figure 29.

Figure 29

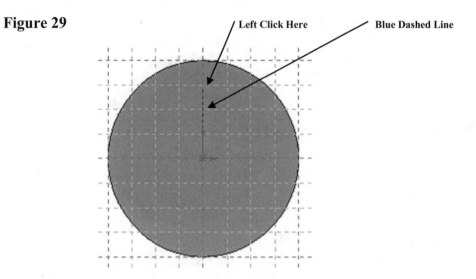

Left Click Here   Blue Dashed Line

33.   Move the cursor to the right side. A circle will form. Let click once as shown in Figure 30.

Figure 30

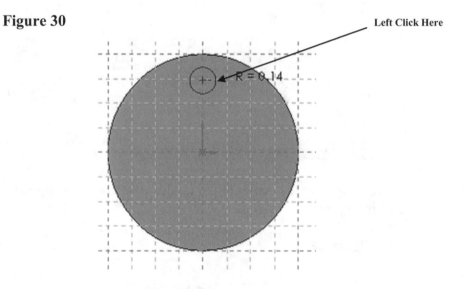

Left Click Here

34. Right click anywhere on the drawing. A pop up menu will appear. Left click on **Select** as shown in Figure 31.

Figure 31

Left Click Here

35. Move the cursor to the upper left portion of the screen and left click on **Smart Dimension** as shown in Figure 32.

Figure 32

Left Click Here

36. Move the cursor over the edge (not center) of the circle until it turns red as shown in Figure 33. Select the circle by left clicking anywhere on the edge. The dimension will be attached to the cursor.

Figure 33

Turned Red

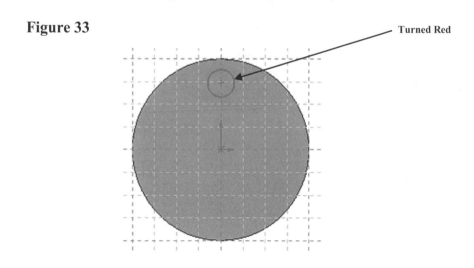

37. Move the cursor to where the dimension will be placed and left click once as shown in Figure 34.

Figure 34

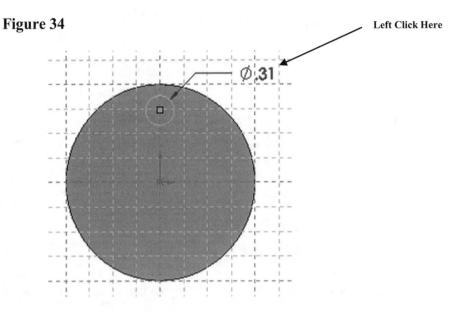

Left Click Here

38. The Modify dialog box will appear as shown in Figure 35.

Figure 35

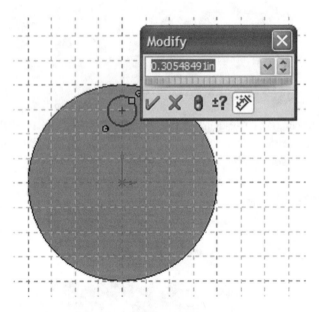

39. To edit the dimension, type **.375** in the Modify dialog box (while the current dimension is highlighted) and left click on the green check mark as shown in Figure 36.

Figure 36

Enter .375 Here   Left Click Here

40. The dimension of the circle will become .375 inches as shown in Figure 37. Use the Zoom icons to zoom out if necessary.

Figure 37

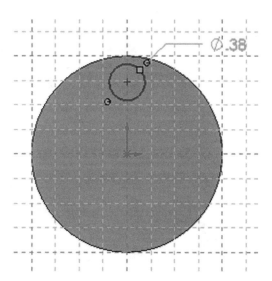

217

41.   Right click anywhere around the drawing. A pop up menu will appear. Left click on **Select** as shown in Figure 38.

Figure 38

42.   After you have verified that no commands are active, right click anywhere on the sketch. A pop up menu will appear. Left click on the **Exit Sketch icon** as shown in Figure 39.

Figure 39

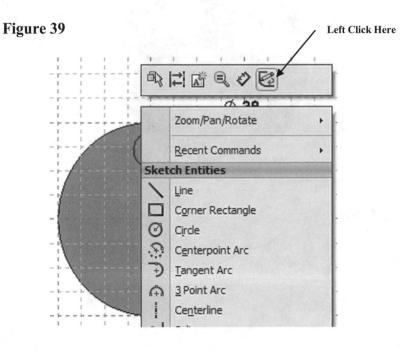

43.   SolidWorks is now out of the Sketch commands and into the Features commands. Notice that the commands at the top of the screen are now different. To work in the Features commands a sketch must be present and have no opens (non-connected lines). If there are any opens in the sketch an error message will appear. Your screen should look similar to Figure 40.

Figure 40

44.   Move the cursor to the upper right portion of the screen and left click on the drop down arrow next to the "Views Orientation" icon. A drop down menu will appear. Left click on **Trimetric** as shown in Figure 41.

Figure 41

Left Click Here

45. The view will become trimetric as shown in Figure 42.

Figure 42

46. Move the cursor to the upper middle portion of the screen and left click on **Extruded Cut** as shown in Figure 43.

Figure 43

Left Click

47. A preview of the cut extrusion will be displayed. If a preview is not displayed left click on the edge of the circle. SolidWorks gave you an error message, there are opens (non-connected lines) somewhere on the sketch. Check each intersection for opens by using the Extend and Trim commands. Your screen should look similar to Figure 44.

Figure 44

48. Enter **.25** next to D1 as shown in Figure 45.

Figure 45

Enter .25 Here

49. Move the cursor to the upper left portion of the screen and left click on the green checkmark as shown in Figure 46.

Figure 46

Left Click Here

50. Your screen should look similar to Figure 47. You may have to use the zoom out command to view the part.

Figure 47

51. Move the cursor to the upper right portion of the screen and left click on the double arrow under Reference Geometry as shown in Figure 48.

Figure 48

52. A drop down menu will appear. Left click on **Axis** as shown in Figure 49.

Figure 49

53. Move the cursor to the side of the part causing both edges to turn red. Left click once as shown in Figure 50.

Figure 50

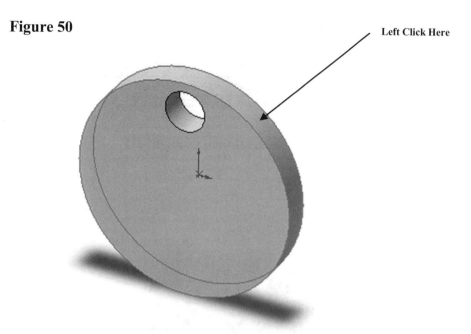

Left Click Here

54. SolidWorks will project a center axis as shown in Figure 51. This axis will be used when creating a circular pattern.

Figure 51

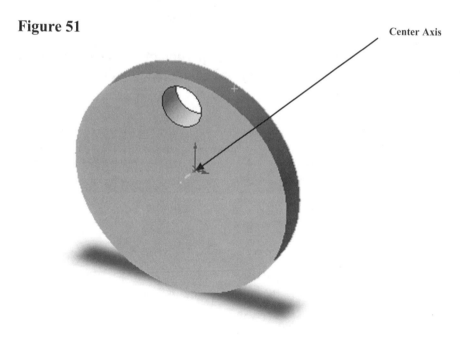

Center Axis

55. Move the cursor to the middle portion of the screen and left click on the green checkmark as shown in Figure 52.

Figure 52

Left Click Here

56. The axis will be displayed as shown in Figure 53.

Figure 53

Center Axis

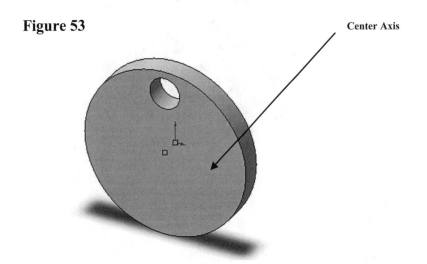

57. Move the cursor to the upper middle portion of the screen and left click on the drop down arrow under Linear Pattern. A drop down menu will appear. Left click on **Circular Pattern** as shown in Figure 54.

Figure 54

Left Click Here

58.   Move the cursor to the left portion of the screen and enter **3** for the number of holes and left click in the box next to the text "Equal spacing" as shown in Figure 55.

Figure 55

Enter 3 Here   Left Click Here

59.   Move the cursor to the center of the circle (hole) as shown in Figure 56. The edges will become red lines. SolidWorks will only find the circle (hole) if the view is trimetric or isometric.

Figure 56   Left Click Here

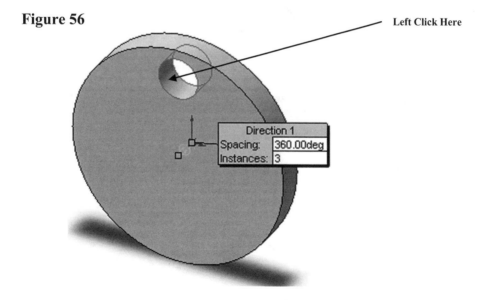

60.   Left click inside the circle (hole). The inside of the hole will turn green. A preview of the holes will be displayed as shown in Figure 57.

Figure 57

61.   Move the cursor to the left portion of the screen and left click on the green checkmark as shown in Figure 58.

Figure 58

62.   Your screen should look similar to Figure 59.

Figure 59

63. Move the cursor to the upper middle portion of the screen and left click the drop down arrow under Fillet. A drop menu will appear. Left click on **Chamfer** as shown in Figure 60.

Figure 60

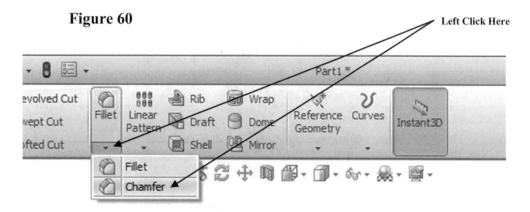

64. Enter **.0625** for the distance as shown in Figure 61. Left click next to Full Preview. Press **Enter** on the keyboard.

Figure 61

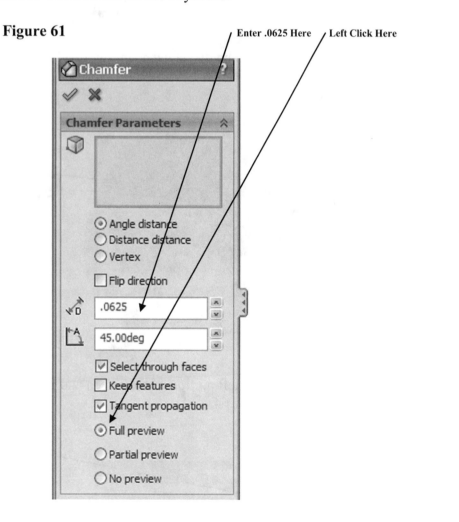

65. Move the cursor over the edge of the part causing it to turn red as shown in Figure 62. Left click once.

Figure 62

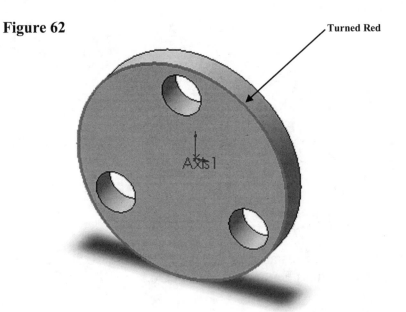

66. A preview of the chamfer will be displayed as in Figure 63.

Figure 63

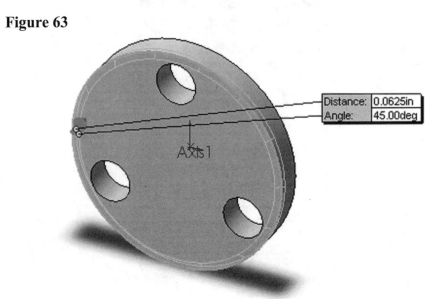

67. Move the cursor to the upper left portion of the screen and left click on the green checkmark as shown in Figure 64.

Figure 64

68. Your screen should look similar to Figure 65.

Figure 65

69. If for some reason a change needs to be made to this part, it can be accomplished by either editing a sketch or feature located in the Part Tree at the middle left corner of the screen as shown in Figure 66.

Figure 66

70.   The Part Tree is shown in Figure 67. Left click on each of the "plus" signs in the part tree. The tree will expand showing more details for part construction.

Figure 67

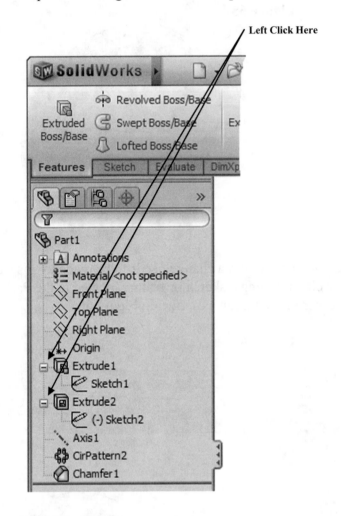

71. Move the cursor over the text "Sketch1". The text will become highlighted as shown in Figure 68.

Figure 68

Highlighted Text

72. The original sketch will also appear as shown in Figure 69.

Figure 69

Original Sketch

73. Right click on **Sketch1**. A pop up menu will appear. Left click on the **Edit Sketch** icon as shown in Figure 70.

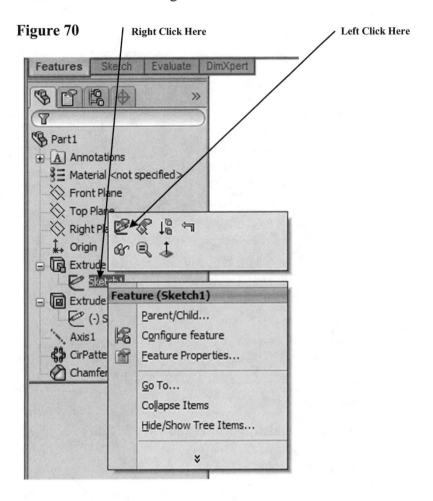

Figure 70

74. The original sketch will appear as shown in Figure 71.

Figure 71

75. Move the cursor to the upper middle portion of the screen and left click on the drop down arrow next to the "Views Orientation " icon. A drop down menu will appear. Left click on **Front** or **Normal To** as shown in Figure 72.

Figure 72

Left Click Here

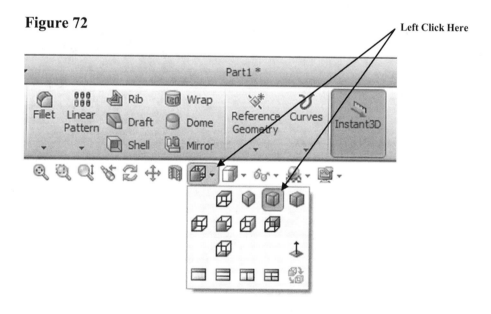

76.   A perpendicular view of the sketch will be displayed. The sketch will look similar to when the sketch was first constructed. Your screen should look similar to Figure 73.

Figure 73

77.   Start by modifying the diameter of the part. Double click on the overall dimension. The Modify dialog box will appear as shown in Figure 74.

Figure 74

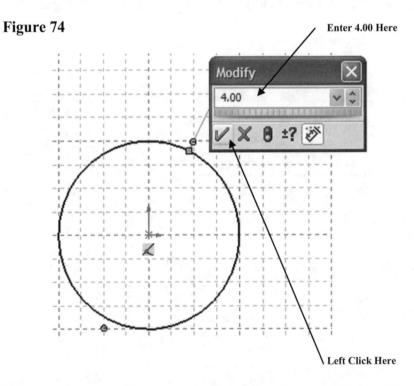

Enter 4.00 Here

Left Click Here

78.   Enter **4.00** and left click on the green checkmark as shown in Figure 74.

79. The diameter of the part will increase to 4.00 as shown in Figure 75.

Figure 75

80. Move the cursor to the upper middle portion of the screen and left click on the green checkmark as shown in Figure 76.

Figure 76

Left Click Here

81. Right click anywhere on the screen. A pop up menu will appear. Left click on the **Exit Sketch** icon as shown in Figure 77.

Figure 77

Left Click Here

82. SolidWorks will automatically update the part to reflect the changes made in the sketch. It will not be necessary to extrude the part again. Your screen should look similar to Figure 78.

Figure 78

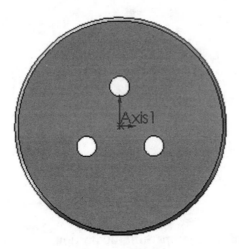

83. Move the cursor to the upper middle portion of the screen and left click on the drop down arrow next to the "View Orientation " icon. A drop down menu will appear. Left click on the **Trimetric** icon as shown in Figure 79.

Figure 79

Left Click Here

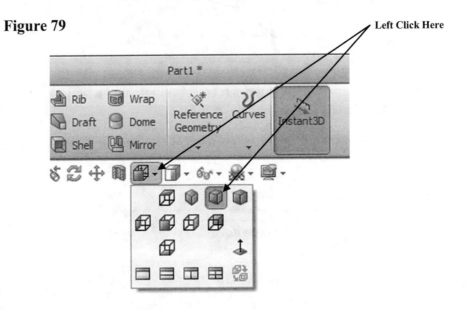

84. Your screen should look similar to Figure 80.

Figure 80

85. Move the cursor to the middle left portion of the screen where the part tree is located. Right click once on **Extrude1**. A pop up menu will appear. Left click on the **Edit Feature** icon as shown in Figure 81.

Figure 81

86. Move the cursor to the middle left portion of the screen. The Extrude1 dialog box will appear. Enter **.750** for the extrusion distance and left click on the green checkmark as shown in Figure 82.

Figure 82

Enter .750 Here   Left Click Here

87. SolidWorks will automatically update the part without the need to repeat any of the steps that created the original part. Notice that the holes are no longer "thru" holes. Your screen should look similar to Figure 83.

Figure 83

No Longer Thru Holes

88. Move the cursor to the middle left portion of the screen where the part tree is located. Right click once on **Sketch2**. A pop up menu will appear. Left click on the **Edit Sketch** icon as shown in Figure 84.

Figure 84

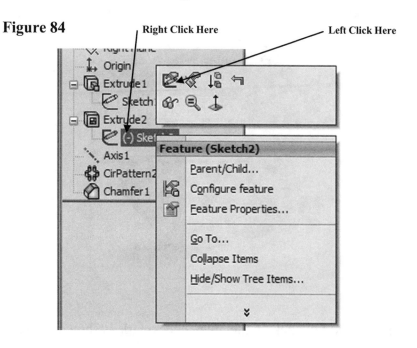

89. The original sketch will appear as shown in Figure 85.

Figure 85

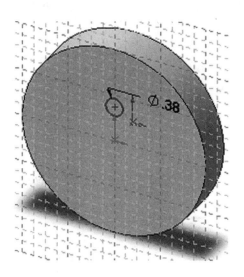

90. Double click on the hole diameter dimension. The Modify dialog box will appear as shown in Figure 86.

Figure 86

Enter .125 Here

Left Click Here

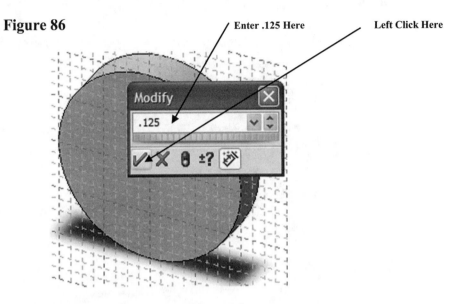

91. Enter **.125** and left click on the green checkmark as shown in Figure 86.

92. The diameter of the holes will be reduced to .125 as shown in Figure 87.

Figure 87

Hole Diameter Reduced to .125

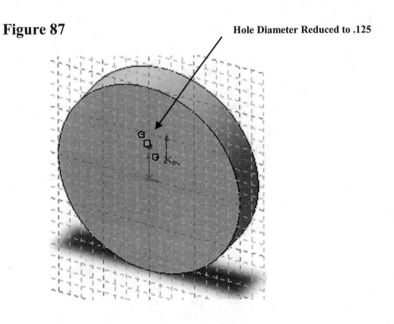

93.   Move the cursor to the upper left portion of the screen and left click on the green checkmark as shown in Figure 88.

Figure 88

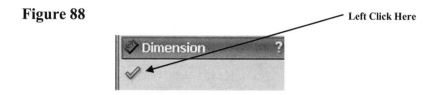

94.   Right click anywhere around the drawing. A pop up menu will appear. Left click on the **Exit Sketch** icon as shown in Figure 89.

Figure 89

95. SolidWorks will automatically update the part as shown in Figure 90.

Figure 90

96. Move the cursor to the middle left portion of the screen where the part tree is located. Right click on **Extrude2**. A pop up menu will appear. Left click on the **Edit Feature** icon as shown in Figure 91.

Figure 91

97.   Enter **.750** of the extrusion distance as shown in Figure 92.

Figure 92

Enter .750 Here

98.   Move the cursor to the upper left portion of the screen and left click on the green checkmark as shown in Figure 93.

Figure 93

Left Click Here

99.   SolidWorks will automatically update the part. Notice that the holes are now "thru" holes as shown in Figure 94.

Figure 94

100.   Move the cursor to the upper middle portion of the screen and left click on the drop down arrow next to the "Views Orientation" icon. A drop down menu will appear. Left click on the **Front** icon as shown in Figure 95.

Figure 95

Left Click Here

101. A perpendicular view of the part will be displayed. Verify the holes are actually thru holes as shown in Figure 96.

Figure 96

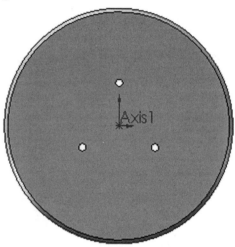

102. Move the cursor to the middle left portion of the screen where the part tree is located. Right click on **CirPattern1**. A pop up menu will appear. Left click on the **Edit Feature** icon as shown in Figure 97.

Figure 97

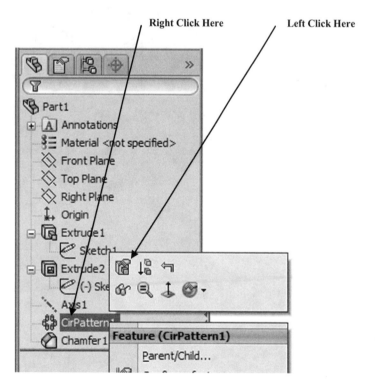

103. Enter **6** for the number of holes and left click next to Equal Spacing as shown in Figure 98. Press the **Enter** key on the keyboard.

Figure 98

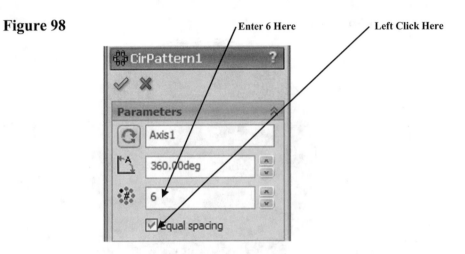

104. A preview will be displayed as shown in Figure 99.

Figure 99

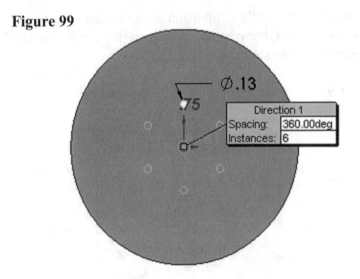

105. Left click on the green checkmark as shown in Figure 100.

Figure 100

Left Click Here

106. Your screen should look similar to Figure 101.

Figure 101

107. Move the cursor to the upper middle portion of the screen and left click on the drop down arrow next to the "Views Orientation " icon. A drop down menu will appear. Left click on the **Trimetric** icon as shown in Figure 102.

Figure 102

Left Click Here

108. The part will be displayed in trimetric as shown in Figure 103.

Figure 103

109. Move the cursor to the middle left portion of the screen where the part tree is located. Right click on **Chamfer1.** A pop up menu will appear. Left click on the **Edit Feature** icon as shown in Figure 104.

Figure 104

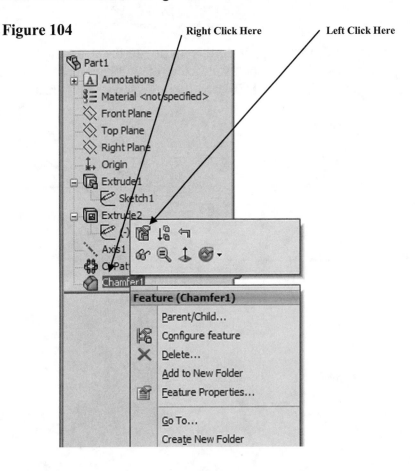

110. Enter **.25** for the Distance a shown in Figure 105.

Figure 105

Enter .25 Here

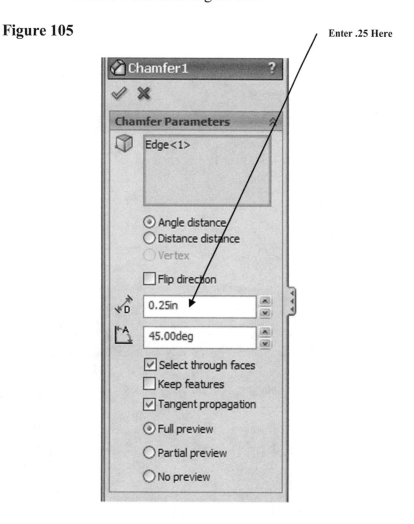

111. A preview of the chamfer will be displayed as shown in Figure 106.

Figure 106

112.   Left click on the green checkmark as shown in Figure 107.

Figure 107

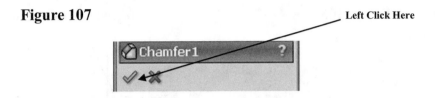

113.   Your screen should look similar to Figure 108

Figure 108

114.   Move the cursor to the middle left portion of the screen where the part tree is
        located. Right click on **CirPattern1**. A pop up menu will appear. Left click on
        the **Suppress** icon as shown in Figure 109.

Figure 109

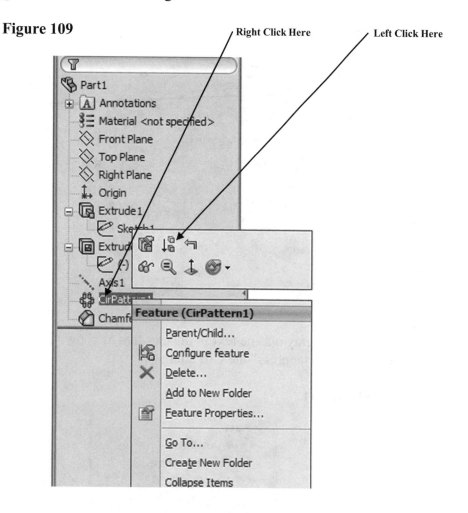

115. All holes created using the Circular Pattern command will be suppressed except for the original hole as shown in Figure 110.

Figure 110

116. SolidWorks will gray out the text in the part tree as shown in Figure 111. Use the same steps to "unsuppress" the CirPattern1.

Figure 111

Text Grayed Out

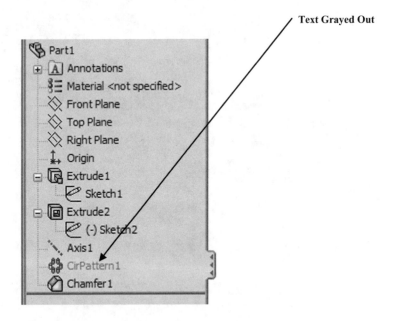

117. The names of all branches in the part tree can also be edited. Left click once on the text **Extrude1**. The text will become highlighted as shown in Figure 112. After the text is highlighted, left click once. The text can now be edited.

Figure 112

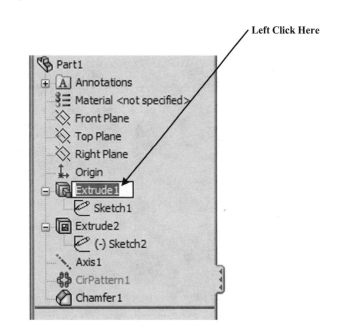

Left Click Here

118. Enter the text **Base Extrusion** as shown in Figure 113. Press **Enter** on the keyboard. Text for each of the individual operations can be edited if desired.

Figure 113

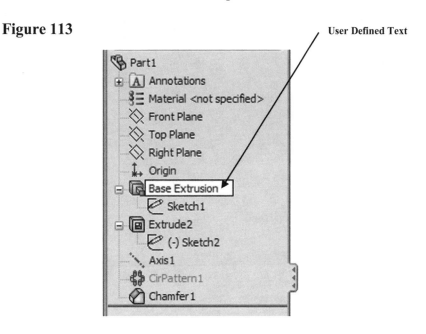

User Defined Text

119. Notice that the final design looks significantly different than the original design. The new part was redesigned by modifying the existing part as shown in Figure 114.

Figure 114

Drawing Activities

Use these problems from Chapters 1 and 2 to create redesigned parts.

Problem 1

Problem 2

Extrude Center Section .25 Deep

Problem 3

Problem 4

Problem 5

Problem 6

Problem 7

Problem 8

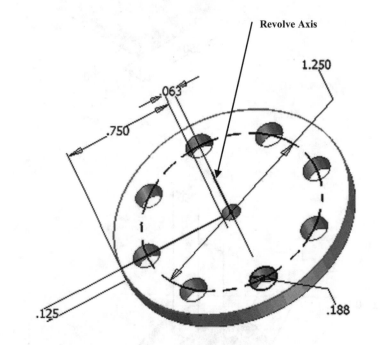

Chapter 6 Advanced Design Procedures

Objectives:

- Design multiple sketch parts
- Learn to use the Front, Top, and Right Planes
- Learn to use the Shell command
- Learn to use the Wireframe viewing command

Chapter 6 includes instruction on how to design the parts shown below.

1.   Start SolidWorks by referring to "Chapter 1 Getting Started".

2.   After SolidWorks is running, begin a new sketch.

3.   Move the cursor to the upper middle portion of the screen and left click on **Circle** as shown in Figure 1.

Figure 1   Left Click Here

4.   Move the cursor to the center of the screen and left click once. This will be the center of the circle as shown in Figure 2.

Figure 2   Center of Circle

5.   Move the cursor to the right and left click once as shown in Figure 3.

Figure 3   Left Click Here

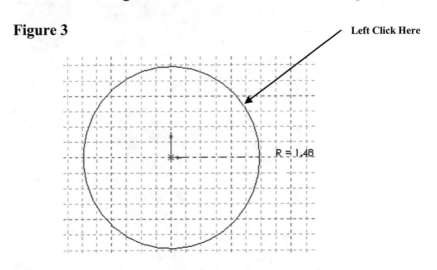

R = 1.48

6. Right click anywhere around the drawing. A pop up menu will appear. Left click on **Select** as shown in Figure 4.

Figure 4

Left Click Here

7. Move the cursor to the upper left portion of the screen and left click on **Smart Dimension** as shown in Figure 5.

Figure 5

Left Click Here

8. After selecting **Smart Dimension** move the cursor over the edge of the circle causing it to turn red as shown in Figure 6. Left click once. The dimension will be attached to the cursor.

Figure 6

Turned Red

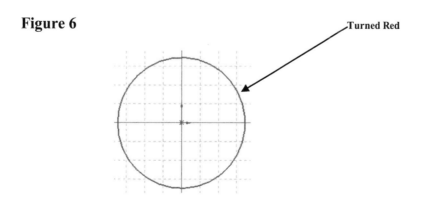

9.   Move the cursor to where the dimension will be placed and left click once as shown in Figure 7.

Figure 7

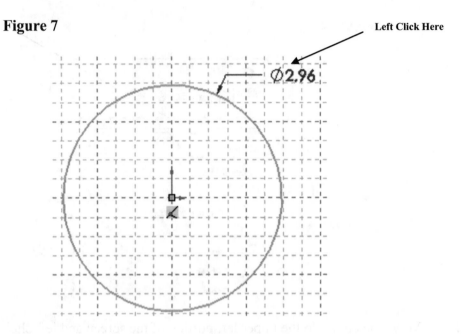

Left Click Here

10.   The Modify dialog box will appear as shown in Figure 8.

Figure 8

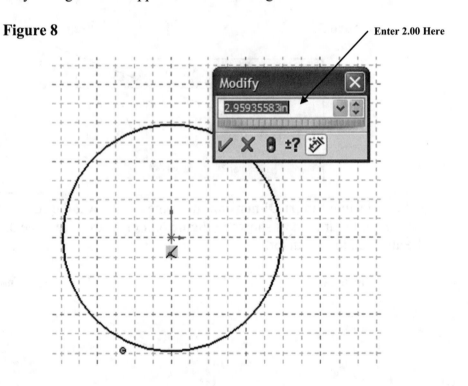

Enter 2.00 Here

262

11.   To edit the dimension, type **2.00** in the Modify dialog box (while the current dimension is highlighted). Left click on the green checkmark as shown in Figure 9.

Figure 9   Left Click Here

12.   The dimension of the circle will become 2.00 inches as shown in Figure 10.

Figure 10

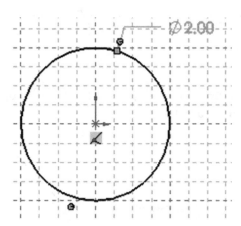

13.   Move the cursor to the upper left portion of the screen and left click on the green checkmark as shown in Figure 11.

Figure 11   Left Click Here

14. In order to view the entire drawing it may be necessary to move the cursor to the middle portion of the screen and left click once on the "Zoom To Fit" icon as shown in Figure 12.

Figure 12   Left Click Here

15. The drawing will "fill up" the entire screen. If the drawing is still too large, left click on the "Zoom In/Out" icon as shown in Figure 13. After selecting the Zoom In/Out icon, hold the left mouse button down and drag the cursor up or down to achieve the desired view of the sketch.

Figure 13   Left Click Here

16. Right click anywhere on the sketch. A pop up menu will appear. Left click on **Exit Sketch** as shown in Figure 14.

Figure 14   Left Click Here

17. SolidWorks is now out of the Sketch commands and into the Features commands. Notice that the commands at the top of the screen are now different. To work in the Features commands a sketch must be present and have no opens (non-connected lines). If there are any opens in the sketch an error message will appear. Your screen should look similar to Figure 15.

Figure 15

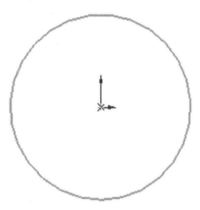

18. Move the cursor to the upper right portion of the screen and left click on the drop down arrow next to the "View Orientation" icon. A drop down menu will appear. Left click on **Trimetric** as shown in Figure 16.

Figure 16   Left Click Here

19. The view will become trimetric as shown in Figure 17.

Figure 17

20. Move the cursor to the upper left portion of the screen and left click on **Extruded Boss/Base**. If the Extruded Boss/Base icon did not appear, left click on the Features tab at the upper left portion of the screen. A preview of the extrusion will be displayed.

21. Enter **2.00** for D1 and left click on the green checkmark as shown in Figure 18.

Figure 18

22. Left click anywhere around the part. Your screen should look similar to Figure 19.

Figure 19

23. Move the cursor to the upper left portion of the screen causing the text "Right Plane" to become highlighted as shown in Figure 20.

Figure 20   Text Highlighted

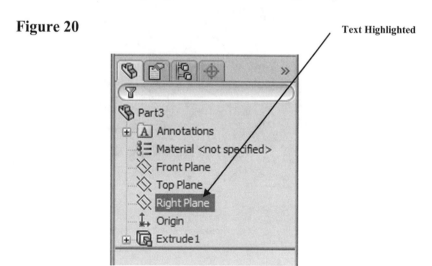

24. The Right Plane will become visible as shown in Figure 21.

Figure 21

25. Right click on the **Right Plane** text. A pop up menu will appear. Left click on **Insert Sketch** as shown in Figure 22.

Figure 22

26. Your screen should look similar to Figure 23.

Figure 23

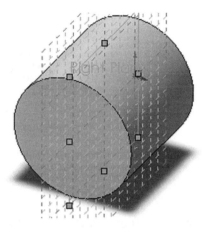

27. Move the cursor to the upper middle portion of the screen and left click on the "Wire Frame Display" icon as shown in Figure 24.

Figure 24

Left Click Here

28. Your screen should look similar to Figure 25.

Figure 25

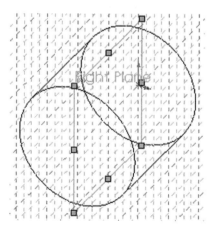

29. Move the cursor to the upper right portion of the screen and left click on the drop down arrow next to the "View Orientation" icon. A drop down menu will appear. Left click on **Right** as shown in Figure 26.

Figure 26

Left Click Here

30. The Right Plane will rotate to a perpendicular view as shown in Figure 27.

Figure 27

31. The lines that make up the part may not be visible. Move the cursor around where they were located. The lines will appear in red. Move the cursor over the top line causing it to turn red and left click once as shown in Figure 28.

Figure 28

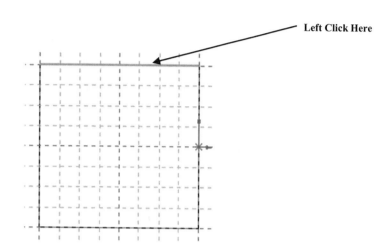

Left Click Here

32. While the line is still green move the cursor to the upper middle portion of the screen and left click on **Convert Entities** as shown in Figure 29. The line will become visible.

Figure 29

Left Click Here

33. Move the cursor over the left vertical line causing it to turn red. Left click once as shown in Figure 30.

Figure 30

Left Click Here

34. While the line is still green move the cursor to the upper middle portion of the screen and left click on **Convert Entities** as shown in Figure 31. The line will become visible.

Figure 31

35. Move the cursor over the lower line causing it to turn red. Left click once as shown in Figure 32.

Figure 32

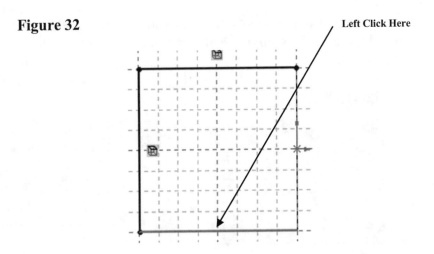

36. While the line is still green move the cursor to the upper middle portion of the screen and left click on **Convert Entities** as shown in Figure 33. The line will become visible.

Figure 33

37. Move the cursor over the right vertical line causing it to turn red. Left click once as shown in Figure 34.

Figure 34

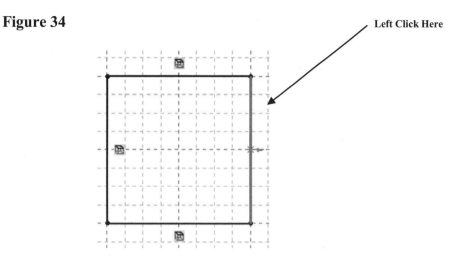

Left Click Here

38. While the line is still green move the cursor to the upper right portion of the screen and left click on **Convert Entities** as shown in Figure 35. The line will become visible.

Figure 35

Left Click Here

39. Your screen should look similar to Figure 36.

Figure 36

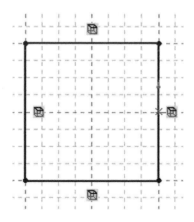

40. Move the cursor to the upper left portion of the screen and left click on **Line** as shown in Figure 37.

Figure 37

Left Click Here

41. Move the cursor to the midpoint of the upper line causing a red dot to appear. Left click as shown in Figure 38.

Figure 38

Left Click Here

42. Move the cursor down to the lower line causing a red dot to appear. Left click as shown in Figure 39.

Figure 39

Left Click Here

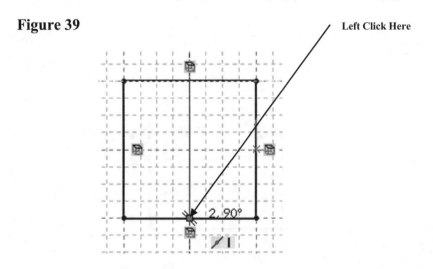

43. Right click anywhere around the drawing. A pop up menu will appear. Left click on **Select** as shown in Figure 40.

Figure 40

Left Click Here

44. Your screen should look similar to Figure 41.

Figure 41

45. Move the cursor to the upper left portion of the screen and left click on **Circle** as shown in Figure 42.

Figure 42

Left Click Here

46. Move the cursor to the midpoint of the center line. A yellow dot will appear. Left click as shown in Figure 43.

Figure 43

Left Click Here

47. Move the cursor out to the side and left click as shown in Figure 44.

Figure 44

Left Click Here

48. Right click anywhere around the drawing. A pop up menu will appear. Left click on **Select** as shown in Figure 45.

Figure 45

Left Click Here

49. Move the cursor to the upper left portion of the screen and left click on **Smart Dimension** as shown in Figure 46.

Figure 46

Left Click Here

50. Move the cursor over the edge (not center) of the circle until it turns red. Left click once as shown in Figure 47.

Figure 47

Left Click Here

51. Move the cursor around. The dimension of the line will appear as shown in Figure 48. The dimension is attached to the cursor.

Figure 48

Left Click Here

52. Move the cursor to where the dimension will be placed and left click once. The Modify dialog box will appear as shown in Figure 49.

Figure 49

Enter .500 Here

53.   To edit the dimension, type **.500** in the Modify dialog box (while the current dimension is highlighted) and left click on the green checkmark as shown in Figure 50.

Figure 50

Left Click Here

54.   Your screen should look similar to Figure 51.

Figure 51

55.   Right click anywhere around the drawing. A pop up menu will appear. Left click on **Select** as shown in Figure 52.

Figure 52

Left Click Here

56. You will need to delete each line that was "converted" (5 total) to the new plane. Move the cursor over each line causing it to turn red. Right click on the line. A pop up menu will appear. Left click on **Delete** as shown in Figure 53.

Figure 53

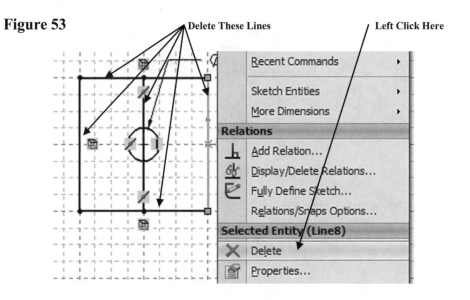

57. Your screen should look similar to Figure 54.

Figure 54

58. Move the cursor to the upper right portion of the screen and left click on the "Shaded with Edges" icon as shown in Figure 55.

Figure 55

59. Your screen should look similar to Figure 56.

Figure 56

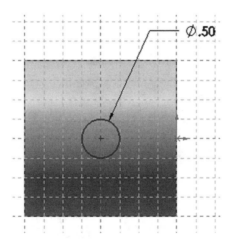

60. After you have verified that no commands are active, right click anywhere on the sketch. A pop up menu will appear. Left click on **Exit Sketch** as shown in Figure 57.

Figure 57

61.   Move the cursor to the upper right portion of the screen and left click on the drop down arrow next to the "View Orientation" icon. A drop down menu will appear. Left click on **Trimetric** as shown in Figure 58.

Figure 58

Left Click Here

62.   Your screen should look similar to Figure 59.

Figure 59

63.   Move the cursor to the upper left portion of the screen and left click on **Extruded Cut** as shown in Figure 60. The Extrude dialog box will appear. Move the cursor to the edge of the small circle causing it to turn red. Left click once.

Figure 60

Left Click Here

64. Move the cursor to the middle left portion of the screen. Enter **1.00** for D1. Left click in the box next to the text "Direction 2". Enter **1.00** for D2 as shown in Figure 61.

Figure 61

Enter 1.00 Here   Left Click Here

65. A preview will be displayed as shown in Figure 62.

Figure 62

66. Move the cursor to the upper left portion of the screen and left click on the green checkmark as shown in Figure 63.

Figure 63

Left Click Here

67. Your screen should look similar to Figure 64.

Figure 64

68. Move the cursor to the upper middle portion of the screen and left click on **Shell** as shown in Figure 65.

Figure 65

Left Click Here

69. Left click on the lower surface as shown in Figure 66.

Figure 66

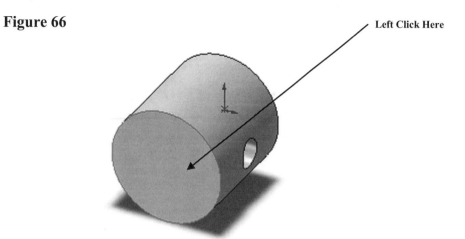

Left Click Here

70. Enter **.10** next to D1. Left click on the green checkmark as shown in Figure 67.

Figure 67

Enter .10 Here   Left Click Here

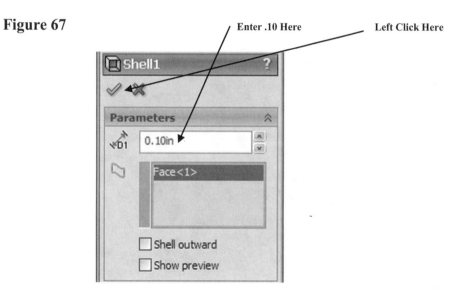

71. Your screen should look similar to Figure 68.

Figure 68

72. Move the cursor to the upper right portion of the screen and left click on the drop down arrow next to the "View Orientation" icon. A drop down menu will appear. Left click on **Front** as shown in Figure 69.

Figure 69

Left Click Here

73. The part will rotate to provide a perpendicular view of the inside as shown in Figure 70.

Figure 70

74. Move the cursor over the same surface causing both the inside and outside lines to turn red. You may have to zoom in for SolidWorks to find both lines at the same time. Both lines must be red at the same time. After both lines are red at the same time, right click on the surface as shown in Figure 71. The surface will turn green.

Figure 71

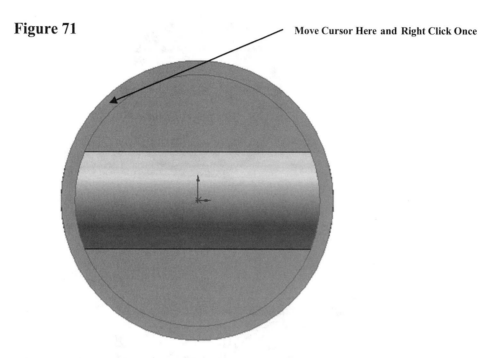

Move Cursor Here and Right Click Once

75. A pop up menu will appear. Left click on **Insert Sketch** as shown in Figure 72.

Figure 72

Left Click Here

76. A new sketch will appear on the selected surface. Your screen should look similar to Figure 73.

Figure 73

77. Move the cursor to the upper left portion of the screen and left click on **Line** as shown in Figure 74.

Figure 74   Left Click Here

78. Move the cursor to the center of the part causing a red dot to appear. Left click as shown in Figure 75.

Figure 75   Left Click Here

79. Move the cursor upward and left click as shown in Figure 76.

Figure 76

Left Click Here

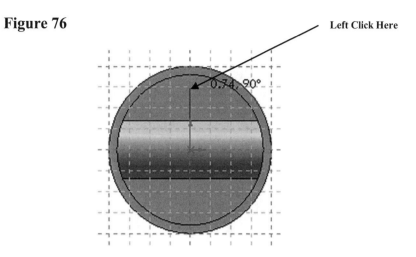

80. Right click anywhere around the drawing. A pop up menu will appear. Left click on **Select** as shown in Figure 77.

Figure 77

Left Click Here

81. Move the cursor to the upper left portion of the screen and left click on **Line** as shown in Figure 78.

Figure 78

Left Click Here

82.   Move the cursor to the center of the part causing a red dot to appear. Left click as shown in Figure 79.

Figure 79   Left Click Here

83.   Move the cursor to the left and left click as shown in Figure 80.

Figure 80   Left Click Here

84.   Right click anywhere around the drawing. A pop up menu will appear. Left click on **Select** as shown in Figure 81.

Figure 81   Left Click Here

85. Your screen should look similar to Figure 82.

Figure 82

86. Move the cursor to the upper left portion of the screen and left click on **Line** as shown in Figure 83.

Figure 83   Left Click Here

87. Move the cursor to the position shown in Figure 84 and left click once.

Figure 84   Left Click Here

88. Move the cursor downward and left click as shown in Figure 85.

Figure 85

89. Move the cursor to the right and left click as shown in Figure 86.

Figure 86

90. Move the cursor upward. Ensure that dots appear from the original starting point. Left click as shown in Figure 87.

Figure 87

91. Move the cursor to the left and left click as shown in Figure 88.

Figure 88

Left Click Here

92. Right click anywhere around the drawing. A pop up menu will appear. Left click on **Select** as shown in Figure 89.

Figure 89

Left Click Here

93. Your screen should look similar to Figure 90.

Figure 90

94. Move the cursor to the upper left portion of the screen and left click on **Smart Dimension** as shown in Figure 91.

Figure 91   **Left Click Once**

95. After selecting **Smart Dimension** move the cursor over the lower endpoint of the vertical line coming out of the center of the part. A red dot will appear. Left click on the endpoint as shown in Figure 92.

Figure 92   **Left Click Here**

96. Move the cursor to the endpoint of the far left line. A red dot will appear. Left click once as shown in Figure 93.

Figure 93   **Left Click Here**

97. Move the cursor upward. The dimension of the line will appear as shown in Figure 94. The dimension is attached to the cursor.

Figure 94

Left Click Here

98. Move the cursor to where the dimension will be placed and left click once. The Modify dialog box will appear as shown in Figure 95.

Figure 95

Enter .375 Here

99. To edit the dimension, type **.375** in the Modify dialog box (while the current dimension is highlighted). Left click on the green checkmark as shown in Figure 96.

Figure 96

Enter .375 Here   Left Click Here

100. The dimension of the line will become .375 inches as shown in Figure 97.

Figure 97

101. Move the cursor to the upper left portion of the screen and left click on **Smart Dimension** as shown in Figure 98.

Figure 98   Left Click Here

102. Move the cursor over the end point of the horizontal line coming out of the center. Left click on the endpoint as shown in Figure 99.

Figure 99

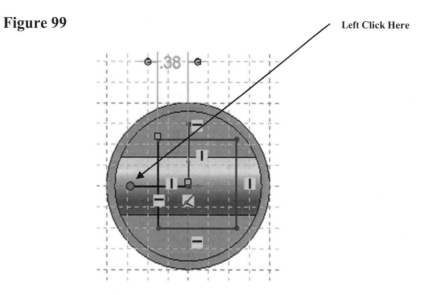

Left Click Here

103. Move the cursor to the endpoint of the upper line and left click once as shown in Figure 100.

Figure 100

Left Click Here

104. Move the cursor out to the side. The dimension of the line will appear as shown in Figure 101. The dimension is attached to the cursor.

Figure 101

105. Move the cursor to where the dimension will be placed and left click once. The Modify dialog box will appear as shown in Figure 102.

Figure 102

Enter .500 Here

106. To edit the dimension, type **.500** in the Modify dialog box (while the current dimension is highlighted). Left click on the green checkmark as shown in Figure 103.

Figure 103

Left Click Here

107. The dimension of the line will become .500 inches as shown in Figure 104.

Figure 104

108. Move the cursor to the upper left portion of the screen and left click on **Smart Dimension** as shown in Figure 105.

Figure 105

Left Click Here

109. Move the cursor over the endpoint of the horizontal line coming out of the center of the part. Left click on the endpoint as shown in Figure 106.

Figure 106

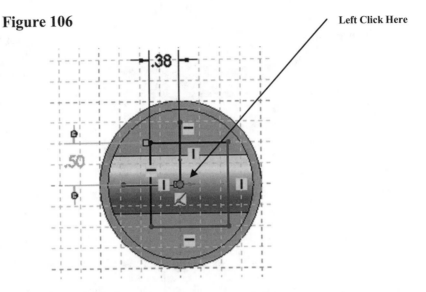

110. Move the cursor to the endpoint of the lower line and left click once as shown in Figure 107.

Figure 107

111. Move the cursor out to the side. The dimension of the line will appear as shown in Figure 108. The dimension is attached to the cursor.

Figure 108

112. Move the cursor to where the dimension will be placed and left click once. The Modify dialog box will appear as shown in Figure 109.

Figure 109

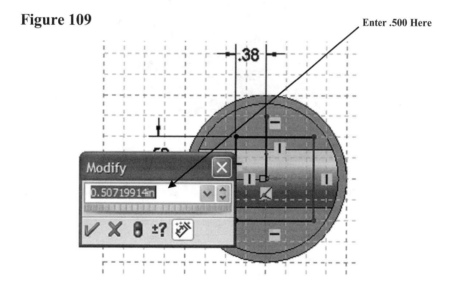

113. To edit the dimension, type **.500** in the Modify dialog box (while the current dimension is highlighted). Left click on the green checkmark as shown in Figure 110.

Figure 110

Left Click Here

114. The dimension of the line will become .500 inches as shown in Figure 111.

Figure 111

115. Move the cursor to the upper left portion of the screen and left click on **Smart Dimension** as shown in Figure 112.

Figure 112

Left Click Here

116. After selecting **Smart Dimension** move the cursor to the upper endpoint of the vertical line coming out of the center of the part. Left click as shown in Figure 113.

Figure 113

117. Move the cursor to the endpoint of the right vertical line and left click once as shown in Figure 114.

Figure 114

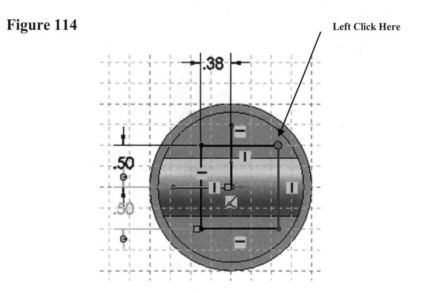

118. Move the cursor out to the side. The dimension of the line will appear as shown in Figure 115. The dimension is attached to the cursor.

Figure 115

119. Move the cursor to where the dimension will be placed and left click once. The Modify dialog box will appear as shown in Figure 116.

Figure 116   Enter .375 Here

120. To edit the dimension, type **.375** in the Modify dialog box (while the current dimension is highlighted) and left click on the green checkmark as shown in Figure 117.

Figure 117

Left Click Here

121. The dimension of the line will become .375 inches as shown in Figure 118.

Figure 118

122. Right click anywhere around the drawing. A pop up menu will appear. Left click on **Select** as shown in Figure 119.

Figure 119

Left Click Here

123. Move the cursor over the vertical line coming out of the center of the part causing it to turn red as shown in Figure 120.

Figure 120

Turned Red

124. After the line has turned red, right click once. A pop up menu will appear. Left click on **Delete** as shown in Figure 121.

Figure 121

Left Click Here

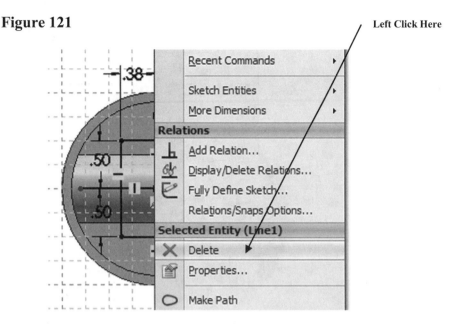

125. Use the same steps to delete the horizontal line coming out of the center of the part as shown in Figure 122. If the dimensions disappear do not be concerned.

Figure 122

Delete This Line

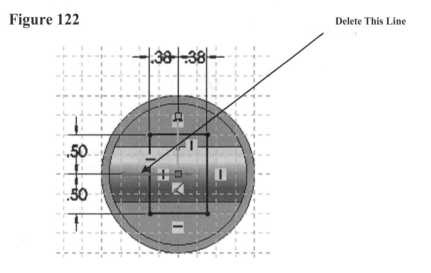

126. Right click anywhere around the drawing. A pop up menu will appear. Left click on **Exit Sketch** as shown in Figure 123.

Figure 123   Left Click Here

127. Move the cursor to the upper middle portion of the screen and left click on the drop down arrow next to the "View Orientation" icon. A drop down menu will appear. Left click on **Trimetric** as shown in Figure 124.

Figure 124   Left Click Here

128. Your screen should look similar to Figure 125.

Figure 125

Left Click Here

129. Move the cursor to the upper left portion of the screen and left click on **Extruded Cut** as shown in Figure 126. If SolidWorks does not provide a preview of the extruded cut, left click on any of the lines that form the box.

Figure 126

Left Click Here

130. Enter **1.875** for D1 as shown in Figure 127.

Figure 127

Enter 1.875 Here

131. Left click on the green checkmark as shown in Figure 128.

Figure 128

132. Your screen should look similar to Figure 129. Use the Rotate command to roll the part around to view the inside.

Figure 129

133. Save the part as Piston1.SLDPRT where it can be easily retired later.

134. Begin a new drawing as described in Chapter 1.

135. Draw a circle in the center of the grid as shown in Figure 130.

Figure 130

136. Use the **Smart Dimension** command to dimension the circle to **.500** inches as shown in Figure 131.

Figure 131

137. Exit the Sketch commands and Extrude the circle to a length of **1.875** inches as shown in Figure 132.

Figure 132

138. Your screen should look similar to Figure 133.

Figure 133

139. Save the part as Wristpin1.SLDPRT where it can be easily retrieved later.

140. Begin a new sketch as described in Chapter 1.

141. Complete the sketch shown in Figure 134.

Figure 134

142. Exit the Sketch commands and change the view to Trimetric. A trimetric view will be displayed as shown in Figure 135.

Figure 135

143. Extrude the sketch to a distance of **2.25** inches. Your screen should look similar to Figure 136.

Figure 136

144. Use the **Fillet** command to create **1.125** inch fillets on the front portion of the part as shown in Figure 137.

Figure 137

Fillet Here

145. Your screen should look similar to Figure 138.

Figure 138

146. Move the cursor to the surface shown in Figure 139 causing it to turn red.

Figure 139

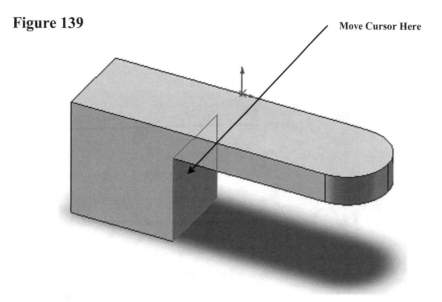

Move Cursor Here

147. Left click once as shown in Figure 140. The surface will turn green.

Figure 140

Left Click Here

148. Right click on the surface. A pop up menu will appear. Left click on **Insert Sketch** as shown in Figure 141.

Figure 141

Left Click Here

149. Move the cursor to the upper middle portion of the screen and left click on the drop down arrow next to the "Views Orientation" icon. A drop down menu will appear. Left click on **Normal To** as shown in Figure 142.

Figure 142

Left Click Here

150. A perpendicular view of the surface will be displayed as shown in Figure 143.

Figure 143

151. Create a sketch on the selected surface as shown in Figure 144.

Figure 144

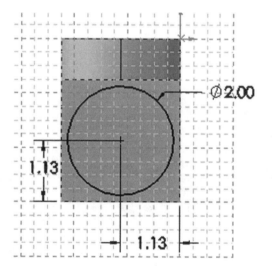

152. Exit out of the Sketch commands and change the view to trimetric as shown in Figure 145.

Figure 145

153. Use the **Extruded Cut** command to extrude or "cut" out (clear through the part) the circle that was just completed. Your screen should look similar to Figure 146.

Figure 146

154. Left click on the top portion of the part causing it to turn green as shown in Figure 147.

Figure 147

Left Click Here

155. Move the cursor to the upper middle portion of the screen and left click on the drop down arrow next to the "View Orientation" icon. A drop down menu will appear. Left click on **Normal To** as shown in Figure 148.

Figure 148

Left Click Here

156. A perpendicular view will be displayed as shown in Figure 149.

Figure 149

157. Draw the sketch as shown in Figure 150.

Figure 150

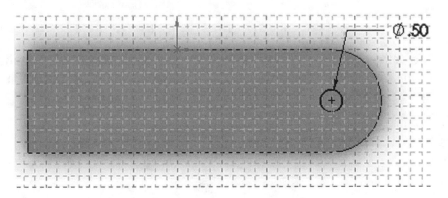

158. Use the **Extruded Cut** command to extrude or "cut" out the circle that was just completed. Your screen should look similar to Figure 151.

Figure 151

159. Change the view to trimetric. Your screen should look similar to Figure 152.

Figure 152

160. Save the part as Pistoncase1.SLDPRT where it can be easily retrieved later.

161. Begin a new drawing as described in Chapter 1.

162. Complete the sketch shown in Figure 153.

Figure 153

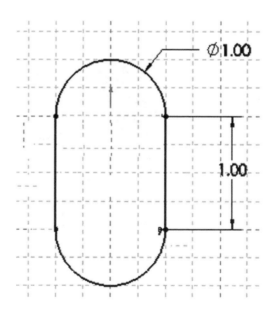

163. Extrude the sketch into a solid with a thickness of **.25** as shown in Figure 154.

Figure 154

164. Complete the following sketch. Use the center of the outside fillet radius as the center of the circle as shown in Figure 155.

Figure 155

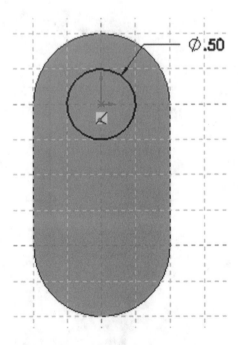

165.   Extrude the sketch into a solid with a thickness of **.25** as shown in Figure 156.

Figure 156

166.   Use the rotate command and roll the part around to gain access to the opposite side as shown in Figure 157.

Figure 157

167. Begin a new sketch on the opposite side as shown in Figure 158.

Figure 158

168. Use the **Normal To** command to gain a perpendicular view as shown in Figure 159.

Figure 159

169. Complete the following sketch as shown in Figure 160.

Figure 160

∅.50

170. Extrude the sketch into a solid with a thickness of **.25** as shown in Figure 161.

Figure 161

171. Save the part as Crankshaft1.SLDPRT where it can be easily retrieved later.

172. Begin a new drawing as described in Chapter 1.

173. Complete the sketch shown in Figure 162. Extrude the sketch into a solid with a thickness of **.25**.

Figure 162

174. Your screen should look similar to Figure 163.

Figure 163

175. Save the part as Conrod1.SLDPRT where it can be easily retrieved later.

176. All of these parts will be used in the next chapter.

Chapter 7 Introduction to Assembly View Procedures

Objectives:

- Learn to import existing solid models into an Assembly
- Learn to constrain all parts in an Assembly
- Learn to edit/modify parts while in an Assembly
- Learn to use the Motion Study command in an Assembly

Chapter 7 includes instruction on how to construct the assembly shown below.

1. Start SolidWorks by referring to "Chapter 1 Getting Started".

2. After SolidWorks is running, begin an assembly drawing. Move the cursor to the upper left corner of the screen and left on **New**. The New SolidWorks Document dialog box will appear. Left click on **Assembly** as shown in Figure 1.

Figure 1

Left Click Here

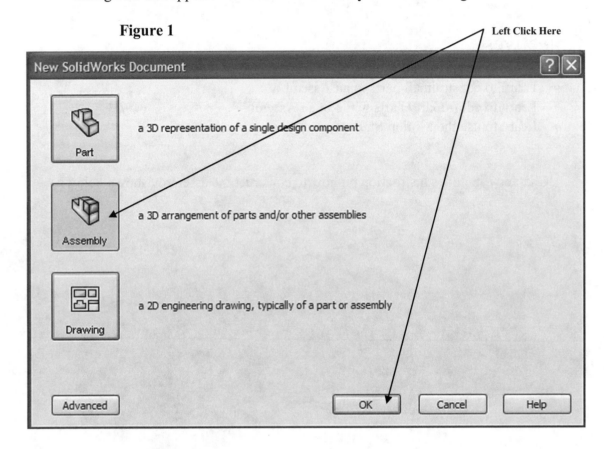

3. Left click on **OK**.

4. The Assembly feature of SolidWorks will open. Your screen should look similar to Figure 2.

Figure 2

5. Move the cursor to the lower left portion of the screen and left click **Browse** as shown in Figure 3.

Figure 3

Left Click Here

6. The Open dialog box will appear. Locate the Case1.SLDPART file and left click on **Open** as shown in Figure 4.

Figure 4

Left Click Here

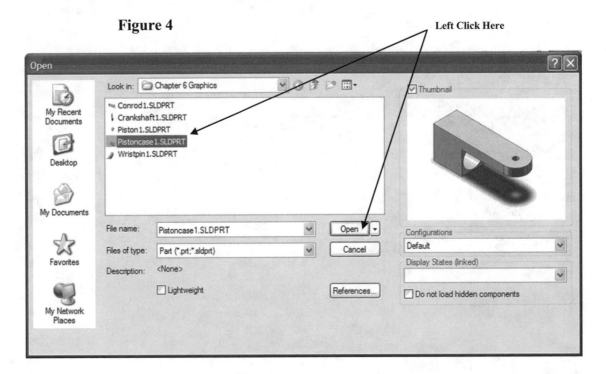

7. SolidWorks will place one piston case in the drawing space. The piston case will be attached to the cursor. The piston case will appear as shown in Figure 5. If the part does not appear attached to the cursor simply left click anywhere in the work area.

Figure 5

8. Left click once. The piston case will be placed in the assembly drawing. Your screen should look similar to Figure 6.

Figure 6

9. Move the cursor to the upper left portion of the screen and left click on **Insert Components** as shown in Figure 7.

Figure 7   Left Click Here

10. Move the cursor to the lower left portion of the screen and left click on **Browse** as shown in Figure 8.

Figure 8   Left Click Here

11. The Open dialog box will appear. Locate the Piston1.SLDPRT file and left click on **Open** as shown in Figure 9.

Figure 9

12. The piston will be attached to the cursor. Place the piston anywhere near the piston case and left click once. Your screen should look similar to Figure 10.

Figure 10

13. Move the cursor to the upper left portion of the screen and left click on **Insert Components** as shown in Figure 11.

Figure 11

Left Click Here

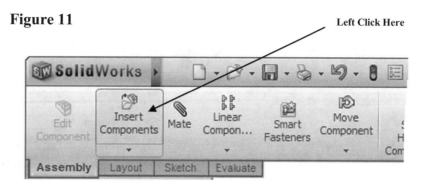

14. Move the cursor to the lower left portion of the screen and left click on **Browse** as shown in Figure 12.

Figure 12

Left Click Here

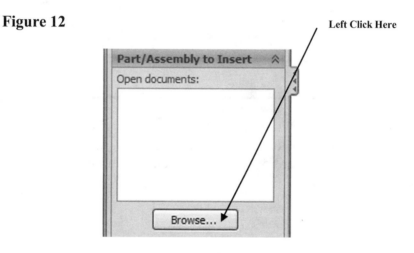

15. The Open dialog box will appear. Locate the Conrod1.SLDPRT file and left click on **Open** as shown in Figure 13.

Figure 13

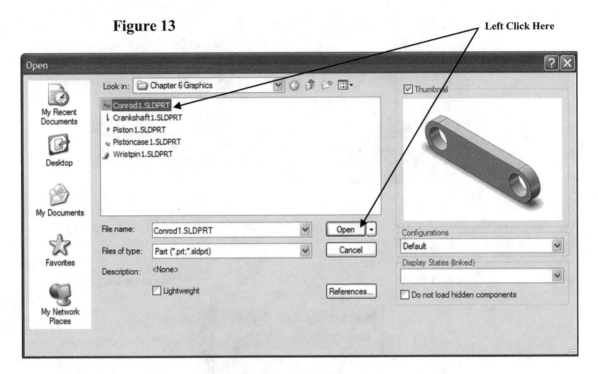

16. The connecting rod will be attached to the cursor. Place the connecting rod anywhere near the piston case and left click once. On the keyboard press the **Esc** button on the key board once. Your screen should look similar to Figure 14.

Figure 14

17.　　Move the cursor to the upper left portion of the screen and left click on **Insert Components** as shown in Figure 15.

Figure 15

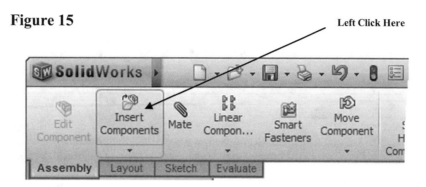

18.　　Move the cursor to the lower left portion of the screen and left click on **Browse** as shown in Figure 16.

Figure 16

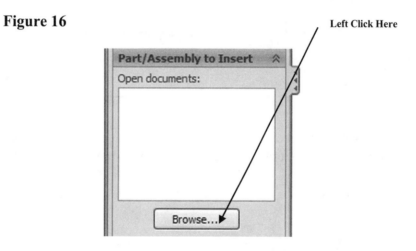

19. The Open dialog box will appear. Locate the crankshaft1.SLDPRT file and left click on **Open** as shown in Figure 17.

Figure 17

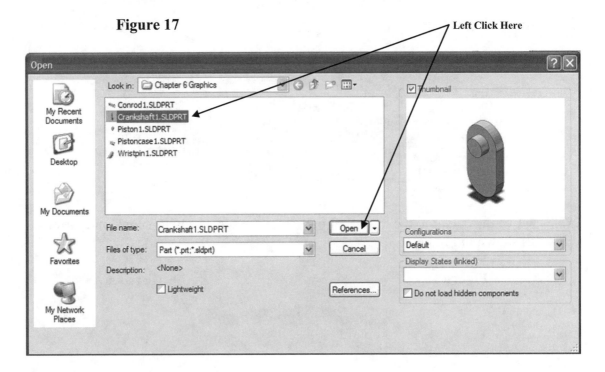

20. The crankshaft will be attached to the cursor. Place the crankshaft anywhere near the piston case and left click once. Your screen should look similar to Figure 18.

Figure 18

21. Move the cursor to the upper left portion of the screen and left click on **Insert Components** as shown in Figure 19.

Figure 19

Left Click Here

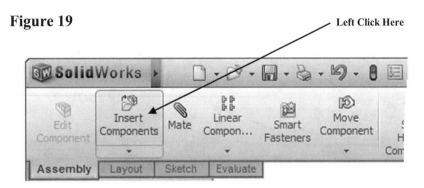

22. Move the cursor to the lower left portion of the screen and left click on **Browse** as shown in Figure 20.

Figure 20

Left Click Here

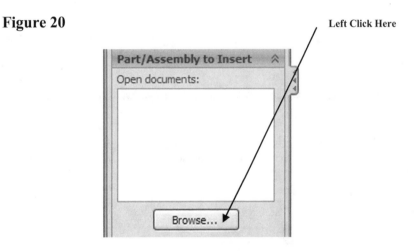

23. The Open dialog box will appear. Locate the Wristpin1.SLDPRT file and left click on **Open** as shown in Figure 21.

Figure 21

Left Click Here

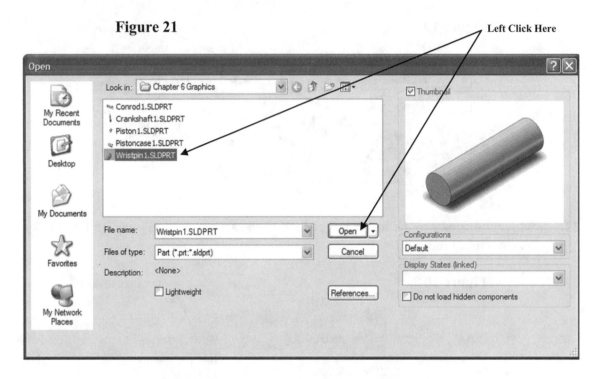

24. The wristpin will be attached to the cursor. Place the wristpin anywhere near the piston case and left click once. Your screen should look similar to Figure 22.

Figure 22

25. The first part inserted into the assembly becomes "fixed" meaning it cannot be moved. All other parts can be moved by left clicking (holding the left mouse button down) and dragging the part to the desired location.

26. Use the **Rotate** command (or press the mouse wheel down) to rotate the entire parts group to the position shown in Figure 23.

Figure 23

27. Move the cursor to the upper middle portion of the screen and left click on **Rotate Component** as shown in Figure 24.

Figure 24

28. Left click (holding the left mouse button down) and rotate the piston to a horizontal position as shown in Figure 25.

Figure 25

Horizontal Position

29. Right click anywhere around the part. A pop up menu will appear. Left click on **Select** as shown in Figure 26.

Figure 26

Left Click Here

30. Move the cursor to the upper left portion of the screen and left click on **Mate** as shown in Figure 27.

Figure 27

Left Click Here

31. Move the cursor to the piston causing the OUTSIDE edges of the part to turn red. Left click once. The part will turn green as shown in Figure 28.

Figure 28

Turned Green

32. Move the cursor to the piston case causing the cylinder edges to turn red. Left click once. The cylinder will turn green as shown in Figure 29.

Figure 29

Turned Green

33. The centers of the piston and the cylinder will be aligned. Your screen should look similar to Figure 30.

Figure 30

34. Left click on the green checkmark beneath the text "Concentric1"as shown in Figure 31.

Figure 31   Left Click Here

35. Left click on the green checkmark beneath the text "Mate" as shown in Figure 32.

Figure 32   Left Click Here

36.   Left click (holding the left mouse button down) and drag the piston down into the cylinder as shown in Figure 33.

Figure 33

37.   Move the cursor to the lower left portion of the piston. Left click (holding the left mouse button down) and slide the piston downward, out below the bore as shown in Figure 34.

Figure 34

38. Move the cursor to the upper left portion of the screen and left click on **Mate** as shown in Figure 35.

Figure 35

Left Click Here

39. Move the cursor to the wristpin hole on the piston causing the inside edge of the hole to turn red. Left click once as shown in Figure 36.

Figure 36

Left Click Here

40. Move the cursor to the upper portion of the connecting rod causing the inside edges of the hole to turn red. You may have to drag the connecting rod to a position where the end holes are accessible. Left click as shown in Figure 37.

Figure 37

Left Click Here

41.   The connecting rod hole and the center of the wristpin hole in the piston will be
        aligned as shown in Figure 38.

Figure 38

42.   Left click on the green checkmark beneath the text "Concentric2" as shown in
        Figure 39.

Figure 39   Left Click Here

43.   Left click on the green checkmark beneath the text "Mate" as shown in Figure 40.

Figure 40   Left Click Here

44. Use the rotate command to rotate the entire assembly around to gain access to the underside of the piston. Move the connecting rod to the location shown in Figure 41. This will take some skill. If the piston moves during this process, use the cursor to move the piston to the original location.

Figure 41

45. Move the cursor to the upper left portion of the screen and left click on **Mate** as shown in Figure 42.

Figure 42   Left Click Here

46. Move the cursor to the left side of the connecting rod causing the edges of the connecting rod to turn red. Left click as shown in Figure 43. You may have to zoom in so that SolidWorks will find the proper surface.

Figure 43   Left Click Here

47. Press the mouse wheel down to rotate the assembly around to gain access to the surface opposite the previously selected surface as shown in Figure 44. Select the second mating surface (while both edges are red) by left clicking as shown in Figure 44.

Figure 44

Left Click Here

48. Left click on the Distance icon and enter **.25** as shown in Figure 45.

Figure 45

Left Click Here   Enter .250 Here

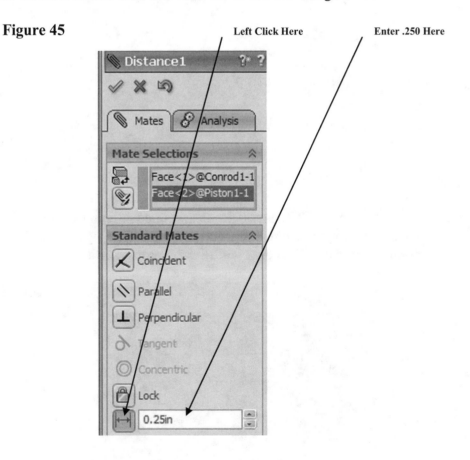

green checkmark beneath the text "Distance1" as shown in

Left Click Here

een checkmark beneath the text "Mate" as shown in Figure 47.

Left Click Here

hould be centered in the piston. Your screen should look
.... to Figure 48.

Figure 48

52. Rotate the entire assembly to the position shown in Figure 49.

Figure 49

53. Move the cursor to the upper left portion of the screen and left click on **Mate** as shown in Figure 50.

Figure 50   Left Click Here

54. Move the cursor to the wristpin causing the edges of the wristpin to turn red. Left click once as shown in Figure 51.

Figure 51

Left Click Here

55. Move the cursor to the wristpin hole causing the edges of the hole to turn red. Left click once as shown in Figure 52.

Figure 52

Left Click Here

56. Left click on the green checkmark beneath the text "Concentric3" as shown in Figure 53.

Figure 53

Left Click Here

57. Left click on the green checkmark beneath the text "Mate" as shown in Figure 54.

Figure 54

Left Click Here

58.   The wristpin will be placed in line with the wristpin hole as shown in Figure 55.

Figure 55

59.   Move the cursor to the upper left portion of the screen and left click on **Mate** as shown in Figure 56.

Figure 56   Left Click Here

60.   Move the cursor to the side of the wristpin causing the edges of the wristpin to turn red. Left click once as shown in Figure 57.

Figure 57   Left Click Here

61. Move the cursor to the side of the connecting rod causing the edges of the connecting rod to turn red. Left click once as shown in Figure 58.

Figure 58

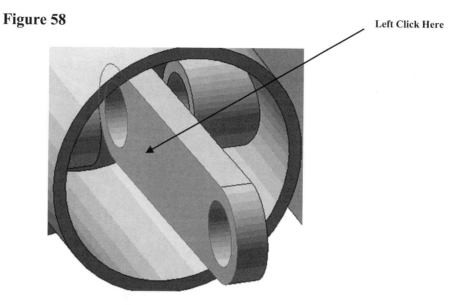

Left Click Here

62. Left click on the Distance icon and enter **.7825**. Left click next to "Flip dimension" as shown in Figure 59.

Figure 59

Left Click Here   Enter .7825 Here

63. Left click on the green checkmark beneath the text "Distance2" as shown in Figure 60.

Figure 60

64. Left click on the green checkmark beneath the text "Mate" as shown in Figure 61.

Figure 61

65. Your screen should look similar to Figure 62.

Figure 62

66. Move the cursor to the upper middle portion of the screen and left click on **Move Component** as shown in Figure 63.

Figure 63

Left Click Here

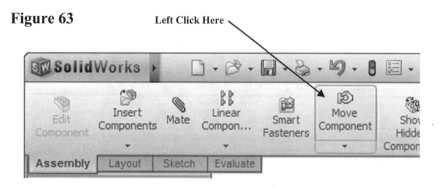

67. Left click again (holding the left mouse button down) and drag the crankshaft to where it can be rotated as shown in Figure 64.

Figure 64

Left Click Here

68. Right click anywhere around the parts. A pop up menu will appear. Left click on **Select** as shown in Figure 65.

Figure 65

Left Click Here

69. Move the cursor to the upper middle portion of the screen and left click on **Rotate Component** as shown in Figure 66.

Figure 66

Left Click Here

70. Left click once. Left click again (holding the left mouse button down) and rotate the connecting rod upward as shown in Figure 67.

Figure 67

Rotate Upward

71. Right click anywhere around the parts. A pop up menu will appear. Left click on **Select** as shown in Figure 68.

Figure 68

Left Click Here

72. Move the cursor to the upper left portion of the screen and left click on **Mate** as shown in Figure 69.

Figure 69

Left Click Here

73. Move the cursor to the crankshaft pin that will secure the connecting rod. The edges of the crankshaft pin will turn red. Left click once as shown in Figure 70.

Figure 70

Left Click Here

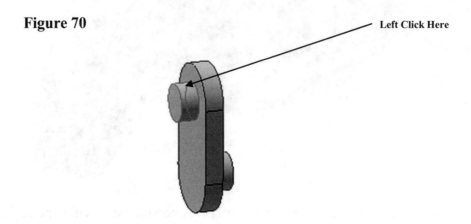

74. Move the cursor to the connecting rod hole that will be secured to the crankshaft. The edges of the connecting rod hole will turn red. Left click once as shown in Figure 71.

Figure 71

Left Click Here

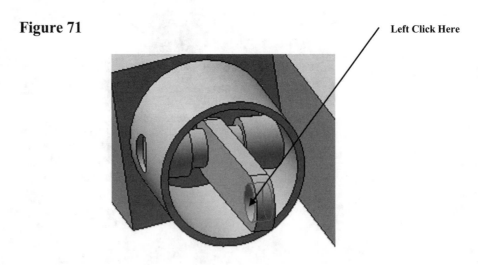

75. Left click on the green checkmark beneath the text "Concentric4" as shown in Figure 72.

Figure 72   Left Click Here

76. Left click on the green checkmark beneath the text "Mate" as shown in Figure 73.

Figure 73   Left Click Here

77. The center of the crankshaft and the center of the connecting rod are now aligned.

78. Left click on the crankshaft (holding the left mouse button down) and drag it to the connecting rod as shown in Figure 74.

Figure 74   Drag Parts Together

79.   Move the cursor to the upper left portion of the screen and left click on **Mate** as shown in Figure 75.

Figure 75

Left Click Here

80.   Move the cursor to the crankshaft pin causing the edge of the pin to turn red. Left click as shown in Figure 76.

Figure 76

Left Click Here

81. Move the cursor to the connecting rod side. The edge of the connecting rod will turn red. Left click as shown in Figure 77.

Figure 77

Left Click Here

82. Left click on the green checkmark beneath the text "Coincident3" as shown in Figure 78.

Figure 78

Left Click Here

83. Left click on the green checkmark beneath the text "Mate" as shown in Figure 79.

Figure 79

Left Click Here

84. SolidWorks will place the connecting rod and crankshaft together as shown in Figure 80.

Figure 80

85. Use the rotate command and roll the assembly around to gain access to the opposite side as shown in Figure 81.

Figure 81

86. Move the cursor to the upper left portion of the screen and left click on **Mate** as shown in Figure 82.

Figure 82   Left Click Here

87. Move the cursor to the crankshaft pin that will be secured in the piston case. The edges of the pin will turn red. Left click once as shown in Figure 83.

Figure 83

Left Click Here

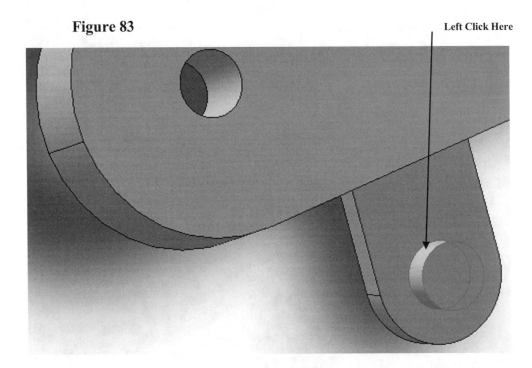

88. Move the cursor to the piston case hole that will secure the crankshaft. The edges of the hole will turn red. Left click once as shown in Figure 84.

Figure 84

Left Click Here

89. SolidWorks will place the crankshaft pin into the piston case as shown in Figure 85.

Figure 85

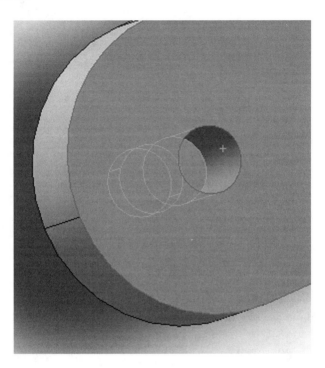

90. Left click on the green checkmark beneath the text "Concentric5" as shown in Figure 86.

Figure 86

Left Click Here

91. Left click on the green checkmark beneath the text "Mate" as shown in Figure 87.

Figure 87

Left Click Here

92. Your screen should look similar to Figure 88.

Figure 88

93. Rotate the parts around to view the assembly. Your screen should look similar to Figure 89. Save the file at this time.

Figure 89

94. The length of the connecting rod must be modified. Move the cursor over the connecting rod as shown in Figure 90. The edges will turn red.

Figure 90

Move Cursor Here

95. Left click once. The surface of the connecting rod will turn green. Right click once. A pop up menu will appear. Left click on **Edit Sketch** as shown in Figure 91.

Figure 91

Left Click Once

Invert Selection

Zoom/Pan/Rotate ▸

Recent Commands ▸

Component (Conrod1)

96. The sketch used to create the connecting rod will be displayed as shown in Figure 92. Use the Rotate command to obtain a better view of the connecting rod.

Figure 92

97. Your screen should look similar to Figure 93.

Figure 93

Double Click Here

98. Move the cursor over the 2.25 dimension. The dimension will turn red. Double click. The Modify dialog box will appear as shown in Figure 94.

Figure 94

Actual Dimension

99. While the text is still highlighted, enter **4.5** and left click on the green checkmark as shown in Figure 95.

Figure 95

Enter 4.5 Here   Left Click Here

100. The length of the connecting rod will become 4.50 inches as shown in Figure 96.

Figure 96

New Dimension

101. Left click on the green checkmark beneath the text "Dimension" as shown as shown in Figure 97.

Figure 97

Left Click Here

102. Right click anywhere around the parts. A pop up menu will appear. Left click on **Exit Sketch** as shown in Figure 98.

Figure 98

Left Click Here

103. Right click anywhere around the parts. A pop up menu will appear. Left click on **Edit Assembly: Assem1** as shown in Figure 99.

Figure 99

Left Click Here

104. The changes made to the connecting rod will be displayed. Your screen should look similar to Figure 100.

Figure 100

105. The length of the crankshaft pin also must be modified. Rotate the assembly to gain access to the backside of the crankshaft as shown in Figure 101.

Figure 101

Move Cursor Here

106. Move the cursor over the crankshaft pin as shown in Figure 101. Ensure that the entire crankshaft pin is highlighted. Left click on the crankshaft pin. The entire pin of the crankshaft will turn green. Right click once. A pop up menu will appear. Left click on **Edit Feature** as shown in Figure 102.

Figure 102

Left Click Here

107. The existing extrusion length will be displayed as shown in Figure 103.

Figure 103

Existing Length

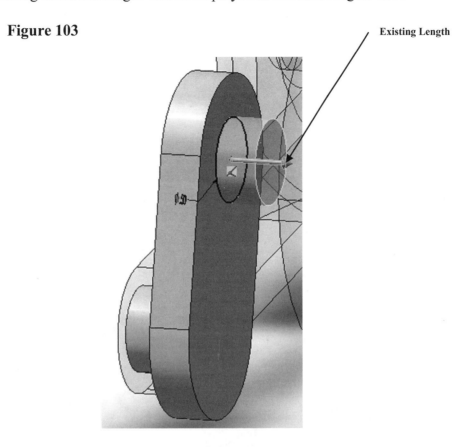

108. Enter **2.00** for the extrusion distance. A preview of the extrusion will be displayed. Left click on the green checkmark as shown in Figure 104.

Figure 104

Enter 2.00 Here   Left Click Here

109. Right click anywhere around the parts. A pop up menu will appear. Left click on **Edit Assembly: Assem1** as shown in Figure 105.

Figure 105

Left Click Here

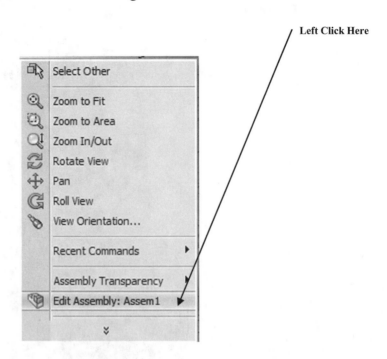

110. The changes made to the crankshaft will be displayed. Your screen should look similar to Figure 106.

Figure 106

111. Rotate the part around as shown in Figure 107.

Figure 107

112. Move the cursor to the lower left portion of the screen and left click on **Motion Study 1** as shown in Figure 108.

Figure 108

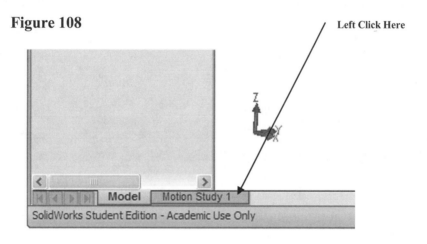

113. The Study Motion dialog box will appear. Your screen should look similar to Figure 109.

Figure 109

114. Move the cursor to the middle right portion of the screen and left click on "Motor" icon as shown in Figure 110.

Figure 110

Left Click Here

115. Move the cursor to the crankshaft pin that protrudes through the piston case. The crankshaft pin will turn red as shown in Figure 111.

Figure 111

Left Click Here

116. Left click once. A red arrow will be displayed showing the direction of motion as shown in Figure 112.

Figure 112   **Left Click Here**

117. Left click on the green checkmark beneath the text "Motor" as shown in Figure 113.

Figure 113   **Left Click Here**

118. Move the cursor to the lower left portion of the screen and left click on the "Calculate" icon as shown in Figure 114.

Figure 114   **Left Click Here**

119.   SolidWorks will begin animating the part. If SolidWorks detects any part collision or interference, the animation will stop playing.

120.   Move the cursor to the lower left portion of the screen and left click on the "Play" icon as shown in Figure 115.

Figure 115   Left Click Here

121.   The Animation can be controlled by increasing or decreasing the speed or looping as shown in Figure 116.

Figure 116   Play From Start   Play   Stop   Speed   Loop

122.   Save the assembly where it can easily be retrieved. When closing SolidWorks, a dialog box will appear indicating that models making up the assembly have been modified. Left click on **Yes** as shown in Figure 117.

Figure 117   Left Click Here

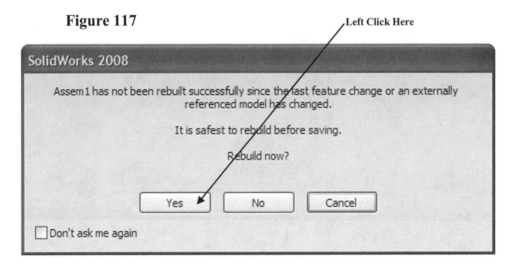

Chapter 8 Introduction to Advanced Commands

Objectives:

- Learn to use the Swept Boss/Base command
- Learn to use the Lofted/Boss Base command
- Learn to use the Plane command

Chapter 8 includes instruction on how to design the parts shown below.

1.   Start SolidWorks by referring to "Chapter 1 Getting Started".

2.   After SolidWorks is running, begin a New Sketch.

3.   Move the cursor to the upper left portion of the screen and left click on
        Line as shown in Figure 1.

Figure 1   Left Click Here

4.   Move the cursor to the center of the screen and left click once. Ensure that the red dot
        appears on the intersection of the origin as shown in Figure 2.

Figure 2   Left Click Here

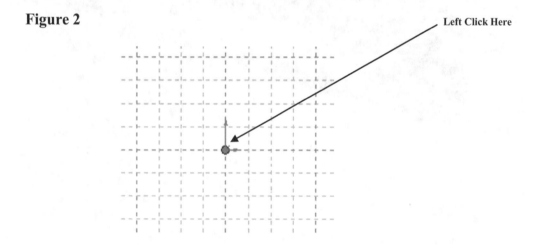

5. Move the cursor to the left portion of the screen and left click once as shown in Figure 3. Right click anywhere on the screen. A pop up menu will appear. Left click on **Select**.

Figure 3

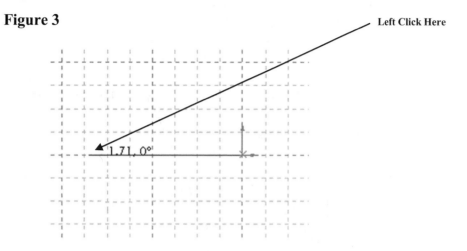

Left Click Here

6. Move the cursor to the upper left portion of the screen and left click on **Line** as shown in Figure 4.

Figure 4

Left Click Here

7.   Move the cursor to the center of the grid and left click once as shown in Figure 5. Move the cursor to the left and left click (draw a short line going off to the left). Move the cursor to the upper left portion of the screen and left click on **Rectangle**. Complete the sketch shown in Figure 5. Be sure to start the rectangle at the origin. After the sketch has been dimensioned, delete the horizontal line that was drawn first. Right click anywhere on the screen. A pop up menu will appear. Left click on **Select**.

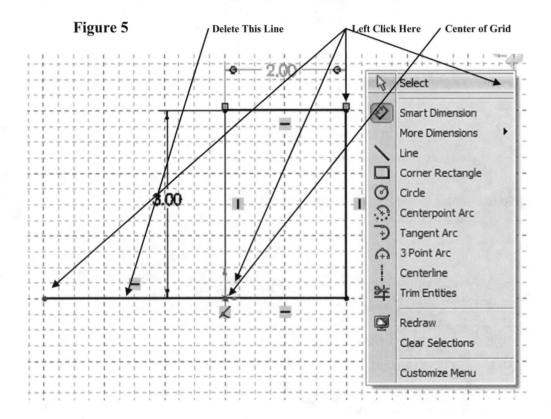

Figure 5

8.   Right click anywhere on the screen. A pop up menu will appear. Left click
      Exit Sketch as shown in Figure 6.

Figure 6

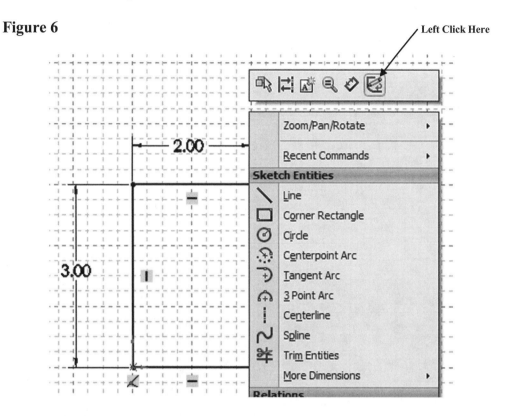

9.   Move the cursor to the upper right portion of the screen and left click on the drop down
      arrow next to the Standard Views icon. A drop down menu will appear. Left click on
      Trimetric as shown in Figure 7.

Figure 7

10. Your screen should look similar to Figure 8.

Figure 8

11. Move the cursor over the text "Right Plane" causing the text to become highlighted. Notice the right plane is highlighted. Right click once. A pop up menu will appear. Left click on **Sketch** as shown in Figure 9.

Figure 9

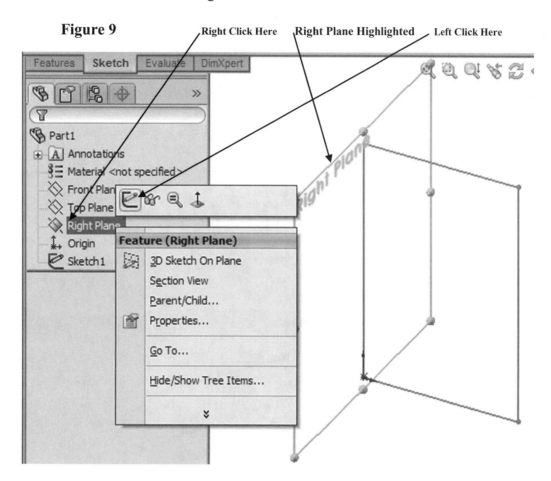

12. Your screen should look similar to Figure 10.

Figure 10

13. Complete the following sketch. Use the Rotate command to provide a better view of the sweep line. The angle of the lines can be estimated. **The sketch lines must intersect with the corner of the 2 inch by 3 inch box as shown in Figure 11**. To dimension on an angle keep the cursor close to the line to be dimensions (while the dimension is still attached to the cursor) then left click once. Press the **Esc** key on the keyboard after completing the dimensioning.

Figure 11   Lines Must Intersect

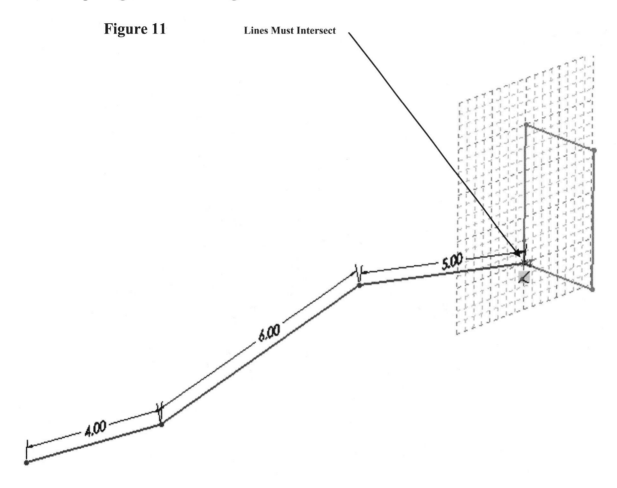

14. Right click anywhere on the screen. A pop up menu will appear. Left click on **Exit Sketch** as shown in Figure 12.

Figure 12

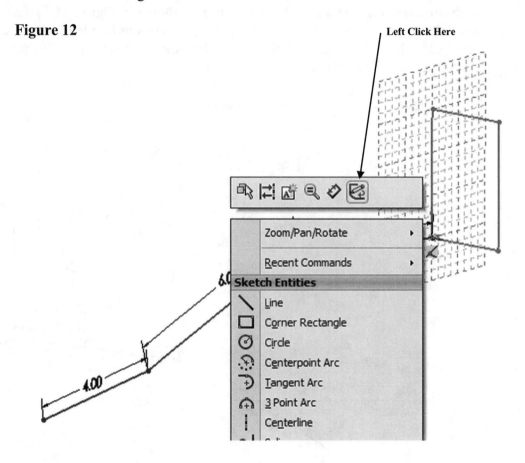

15.   Your screen should look similar to Figure 13.

> **Figure 13**

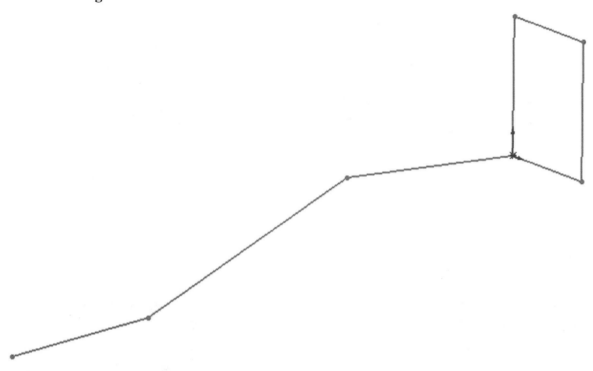

16.   Move the cursor to the upper left portion of the screen and left click on
Swept Boss/Base as shown in Figure 14.

> **Figure 14**

17. Left click on one of the lines that make up the rectangle as shown in Figure 15.

Figure 15

18. SolidWorks will provide a preview of the sweep. Left click on the green check mark as shown in Figure 16.

Figure 16

19. Your screen should look similar to Figure 17.

Figure 17

20. Move the cursor to the upper middle portion of the screen and left click on **Shell** as shown in Figure 18.

Figure 18

21. Move the cursor to the left side face and left click once. Using the **Rotate** command, rotate the part around to gain access to the right side face and left click once as shown in Figure 19.

Figure 19

22.   Left click on the green check mark as shown in Figure 20.

Figure 20

Left Click Here

23.   Use the **Rotate** command to access the ends of the model. The model should be open on both ends similar to a piece of rectangular tubing. Your screen should look similar to Figure 21.

Figure 21

Hollow Tubing

24. Begin a New Sketch.

25. Move the cursor to the upper left portion of the screen and left click on **Rectangle** as shown in Figure 22.

Figure 22

26. Move the cursor to the center of the screen and left click once. Ensure that the red dot appears on the intersection of the origin as shown in Figure 23.

Figure 23

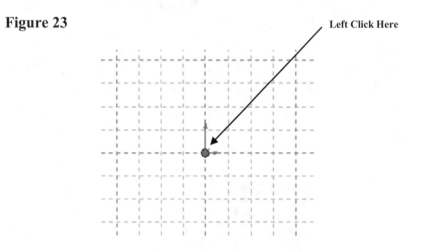

27.   Complete the sketch as shown in Figure 24. Right click anywhere on the screen. A pop up menu will appear. Left click on **Select** as shown in Figure 24.

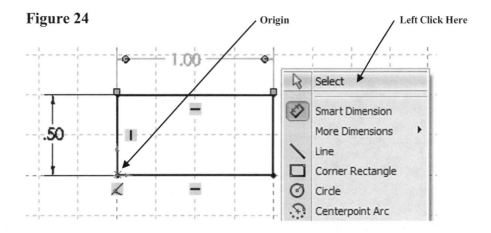

Figure 24

28.   Right click anywhere on the screen. A pop up menu will appear. Left click on **Exit Sketch** as shown in Figure 25.

Figure 25

29.   Move the cursor to the upper middle portion of the screen and left click on the drop down arrow to the right of the Views Orientation icon. A drop down menu will appear. Left click on **Trimetric** as shown in Figure 26.

Figure 26

Left Click Here

30.   Use the **Extruded Boss/Base** command to extrude the sketch to a thickness of .001 of an inch as shown in Figure 27.

Figure 27

31. Move the cursor to the upper middle portion of the screen and left click on the drop down arrow underneath Reference Geometry. A drop down menu will appear. Left click on **Plane** as shown in Figure 28.

Figure 28

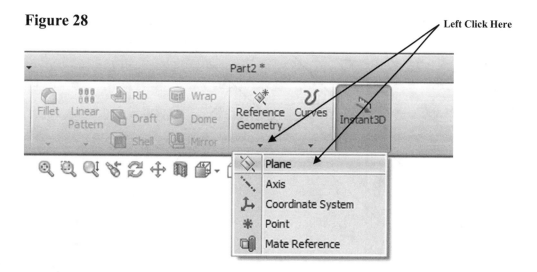

32.   Left click on the surface of the solid. SolidWorks will provide a preview of the
        new plane. Left click on the Distance icon and enter 1.00. Left click on the green
        check mark as shown in Figure 29.

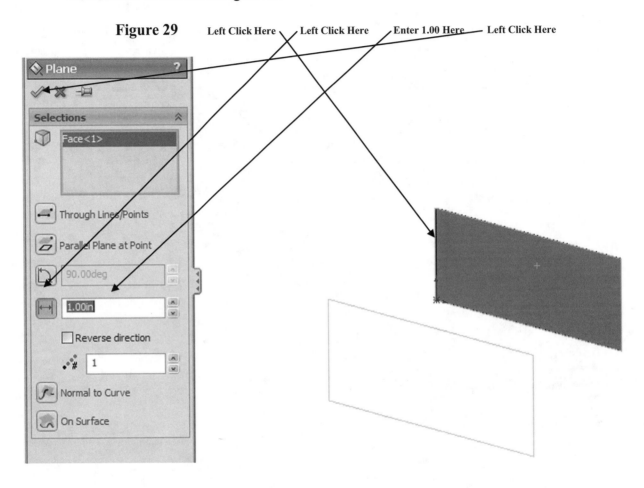

Figure 29   Left Click Here   Left Click Here   Enter 1.00 Here   Left Click Here

33. Your screen should look similar to Figure 30.

Figure 30

New Plane

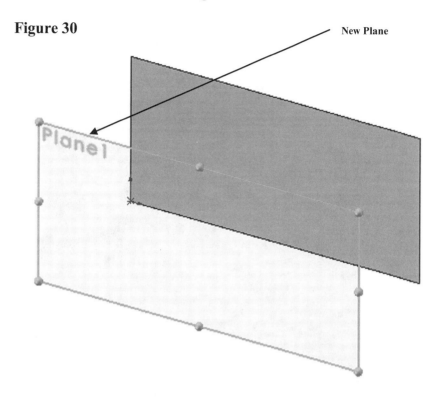

34. Move the cursor to the edge of the newly created plane and right click. A pop up menu will appear. Left click on **Sketch** as shown in Figure 31.

Figure 31

Left Click Here

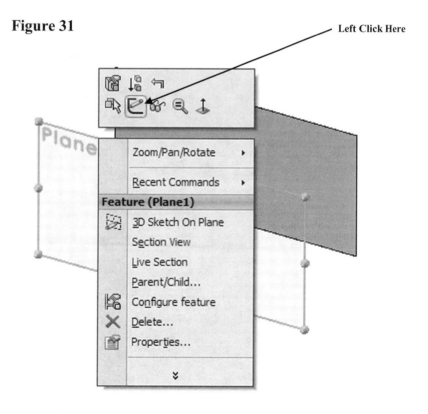

35. A new sketch will appear on the newly created plane as shown in Figure 32.

Figure 32

Newly Created Plane

36. Draw a small rectangle in the corner of the sketch as shown in Figure 33. Estimate size and distance.

Figure 33

Small Rectangular Sketch

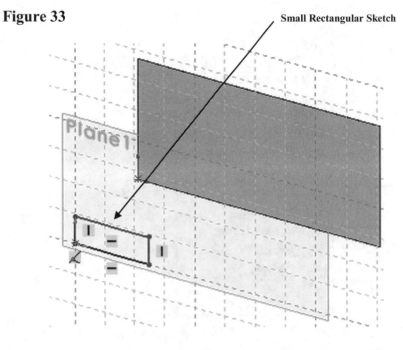

37. Once the sketch is complete, right click anywhere around the part. A pop up menu will appear. Left click on **Exit Sketch** as shown in Figure 34.

Figure 34

Left Click Here

38. Move the cursor to the upper middle portion of the screen and left click on the drop down arrow underneath Reference Geometry. A drop down menu will appear. Left click on **Plane** as shown in Figure 35.

Figure 35

Left Click Here

39. SolidWorks will place another plane 1.00 inch in front of the previous plane. If another plane does not appear, left click on the edge of Plane 1. Left click on the green check mark. Your screen should look similar to Figure 36.

Figure 36

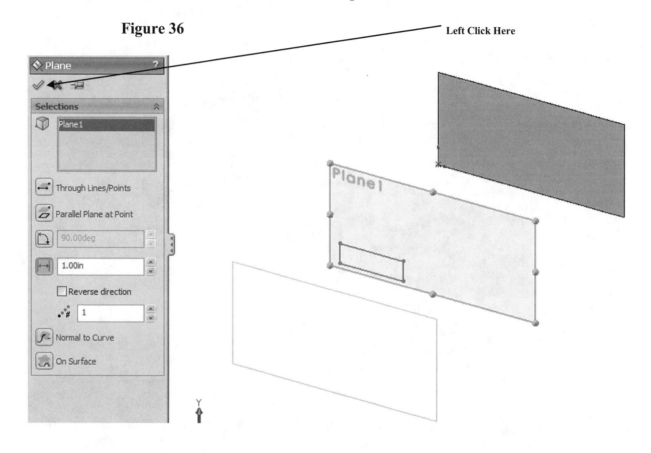

40. Your screen should look similar to Figure 37.

Figure 37

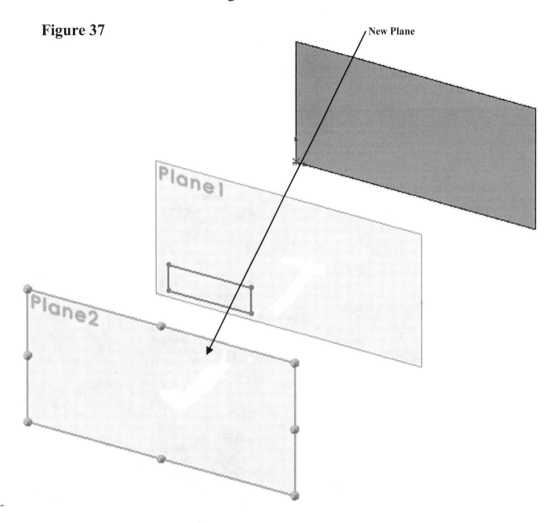

41   Move the cursor to the edge of the newly created plane and right click. A pop up menu will appear. Left click on **Sketch** as shown in Figure 38.

Figure 38

42.   A new sketch will appear on the newly created plane as shown in Figure 39.

Figure 39

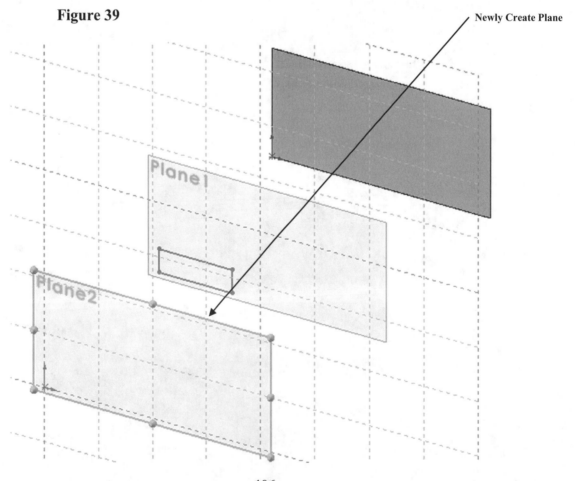

43. Draw a small circle in the corner of the sketch as shown in Figure 40. Estimate size and distance.

Figure 40

Small Circle Sketch

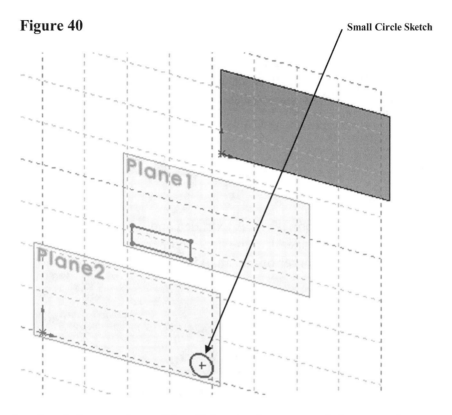

44. Once the sketch is complete, right click anywhere around the part. A pop up menu will appear. Left click on **Exit Sketch** as shown in Figure 41.

Figure 41

Left Click Here

45. Move the cursor to the upper left portion of the screen and left click on **Lofted Boss/Base** as shown in Figure 42.

Figure 42

Left Click Here

46. Move the cursor to the first box that was extruded and left click on the face. Because the Profile banner appears in the upper corner of the first sketch, move the cursor to the upper left corner of the small box (second sketch in the same location) and left click.

Figure 43

Left Click Here

47. Your screen should look similar to Figure 44.

Figure 44

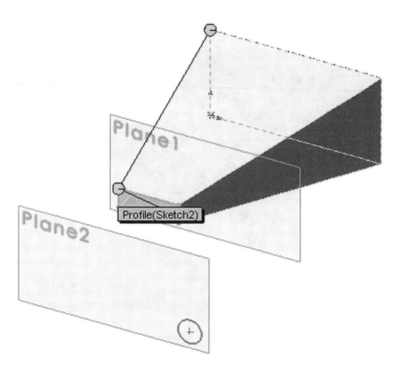

48. Move the cursor to the edge of the circle and left click as shown in Figure 45.

Figure 45

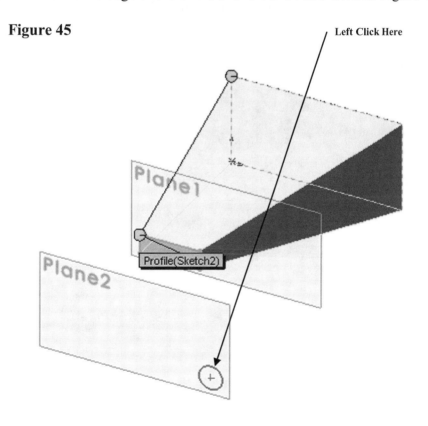

49. Your screen should look similar to Figure 46.

Figure 46

50. Left click on the green check mark as shown in Figure 47. Press the **Esc** key several times.

Figure 47   Left Click Here

51. Your screen should look similar to Figure 48.

Figure 48

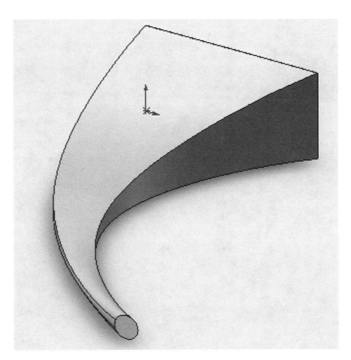

Chapter 9 Introduction to COSMOSXpress

Objectives:

- Learn to create simple parts used to run COSMOSXpress
- Learn to interpret the results of an analysis

Chapter 9 includes instruction on how to run the analysis shown below.

1.   Start SolidWorks by referring to "Chapter 1 Getting Started".

2.   Begin a new Sketch.

3.   Complete the sketch as shown in Figure 1.

    Figure 1

4.   Extrude the sketch a distance of 2 inches as shown in Figure 2.

    Figure 2

5.   Save the part where it can easily be retrieved later.

6.   Move the cursor to the upper left portion of the screen and left click on the arrow to the right of SolidWorks. A drop down menu will appear. Left click on **COSMOSXpress** as shown in Figure 3.

Figure 3

7.   The COSMOSXpress dialog box will appear as shown in Figure 4.

Figure 4

8.   Left click on the **Material** tab. Left click on the plus sign to the left of Aluminum Alloys. The tree will expand. Left click on **1060 Alloy.** Left click on **Apply.** Left click on **Next** as shown in Figure 5.

Figure 5

9.   A description of available material will appear as shown in Figure 6.

Figure 6

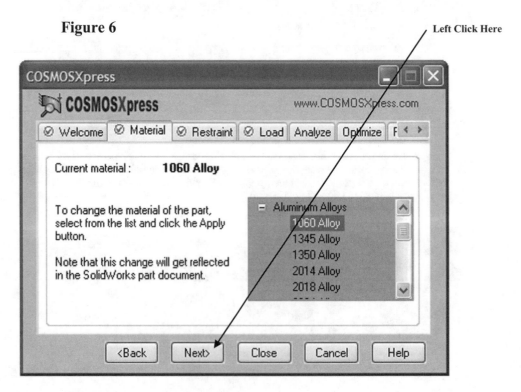

10. The Restraint tab will appear as shown in Figure 7.

Figure 7

11. Rotate the part upward to gain access to the bottom as shown in Figure 8.

Figure 8

12. Left click on the bottom surfaces of the part as shown in Figure 9.

Figure 9

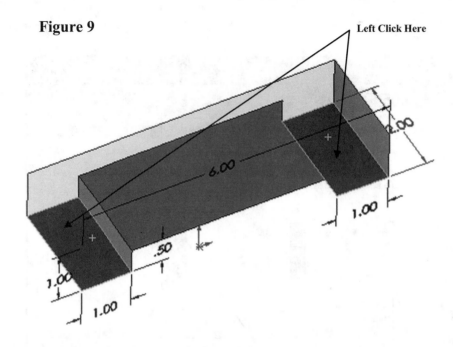

13. Left click on **Next** as shown in Figure 10.

Figure 10

14. Your screen should look similar to Figure 11.

Figure 11

15. Left click on **Next** as shown in Figure 12.

Figure 12

16. The Load tab will be selected as shown in Figure 13.

Figure 13

Already Selected

17. Rotate the part back to its original position as shown in Figure 14.

Figure 14

18. Left click on the top surface as shown in Figure 15.

Figure 15

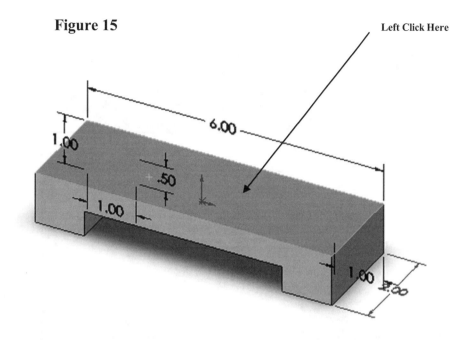

19. Left click on **Next** as shown in Figure 16.

Figure 16

20. Place a dot next to "Force". Left click on **Next** shown in Figure 17.

Figure 17

21. Left click on **Next** as shown in Figure 18.

Figure 18

22. Left click on the arrow to the right of "N" and change the units to **lbs**. Enter **100** for the value as shown in Figure 19.

Figure 19

23. Left click on **Next** as shown in Figure 20.

Figure 20

23.   Place a dot next to "Yes (recommended)". Left click on **Next** as shown in Figure 21.

Figure 21

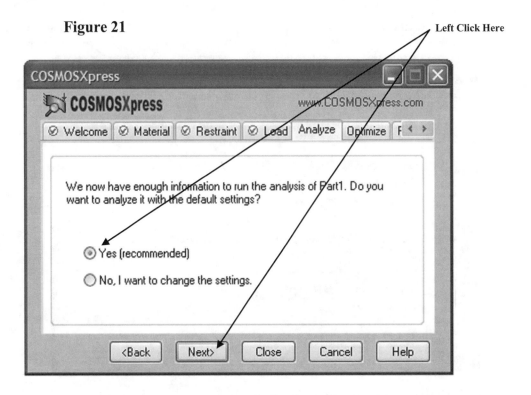

24.   Left click on **Run** as shown in Figure 22.

Figure 22

25. The lowest Factor of Safety found on this part is 15.3447. Left click on **Next** as shown in Figure 23.

Figure 23

27. COSMOSXpress will ask if you want to optimize the design. Place a dot next to **Yes** and left click on **Next** as shown in Figure 24.

Figure 24

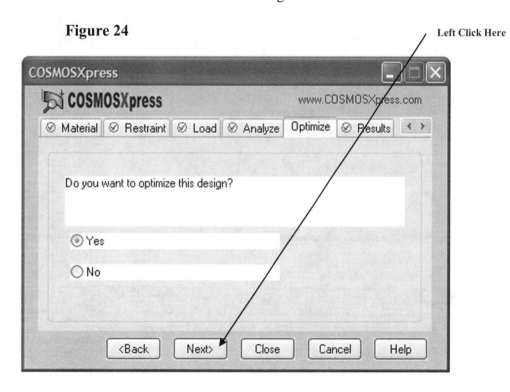

28.   Left click on **Next** as shown in Figure 25.

Figure 25

29.   Left click on **Next** as shown in Figure 26.

Figure 26

30.   Left click on **Next** as shown in Figure 27.

Figure 27

Left Click Here

31.   Left click on **Next** as shown in Figure 28.

Figure 28

Turned Green

32. Place a dot next to "Show me the stress distribution in the model" and left click on **Next** as shown in Figure 29.

Figure 29

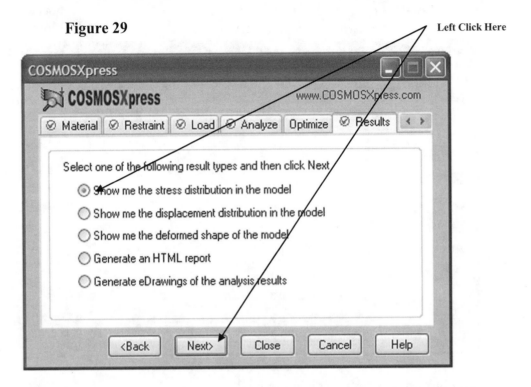

33. SolidWorks will provide an exaggerated display of the stress analysis that was encountered during the test. Your screen should look similar to Figure 30. Rotate the part upward to identify any problems areas in the design. Areas of red indicate a potential high stress area.

Figure 30

von Mises (N/m^2)

4.040e+003
3.707e+003
3.374e+003
3.040e+003
2.707e+003
2.374e+003
2.041e+003
1.708e+003
1.375e+003
1.042e+003
7.088e+002
3.757e+002
4.265e+001

→ Yield strength: 2.757e+007

34.   Left click on **Play** as shown in Figure 31. SolidWorks will provide an exaggerated video of the stress analysis test.

Figure 31   Left Click Here

35.   Left click on **Stop** as shown in Figure 32. Save the file where it can be retrieved later.

Figure 32   Left Click Here

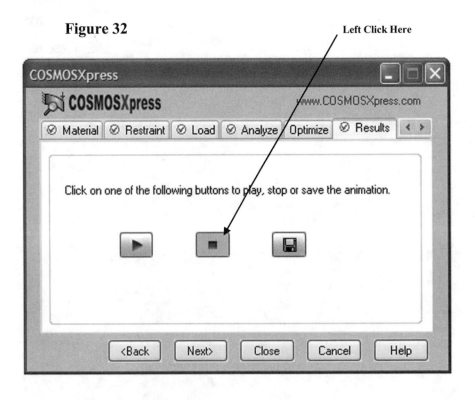

36. Complete the sketch shown in Figure 33.

Figure 33

37. Extrude the sketch to a distance of **96** inches as shown in Figure 34.

Figure 34

38. Use the **Shell** command to shell the part with a distance of **.10** as shown in Figure 35.

Figure 35

Shelled to .01

39. Move the cursor to the upper left portion of the screen and left click on the arrow to the right of SolidWorks. Left click on **Tools**. A drop down menu will appear. Left click on **COSMOSXpress** as shown in Figure 36.

Figure 36

Left Click Here

40. Run an analysis on this part (using **Cast Alloy Steel** for material and **100 lbs** for the Load) using one the left side as the Restraint surface and the top as the Load surface as shown in Figure 37. This will create a cantilever effect for the analysis. If the analysis requires too much memory to run, reduce the length of the part and try again.

Figure 37

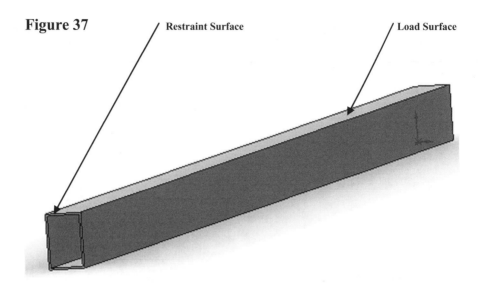

Restraint Surface   Load Surface

41. After the analysis has been run, your screen should look similar to Figure 38.

Figure 38   Restraint Surface   Load Surface

| 4.426e+007 |
| 4.057e+007 |
| 3.688e+007 |
| 3.320e+007 |
| 2.951e+007 |
| 2.582e+007 |
| 2.213e+007 |
| 1.844e+007 |
| 1.476e+007 |
| 1.107e+007 |
| 7.379e+006 |
| 3.691e+006 |
| 3.031e+003 |

→ Yield strength: 2.413e+008

Chapter 10 Introduction to Mechanical Mates

Objectives:

- Learn to create a cam and lifter system of parts
- Learn to use one of the Mechanical Mates options

Chapter 10 includes instruction on how to construct the assembly shown below.

1.   Start SolidWorks by referring to "Chapter 1 Getting Started".

2.   After SolidWorks is running, begin a New Sketch.

Figure 1

3.   Exit the Sketch area. Extrude the sketch to a thickness of **1.00** in as shown in Figure 2

Figure 2

4. Use the **Fillet** command (.5 inch fillets) to radius the lower edge(s) as shown in Figure 3.

Figure 3

5. Use the **Rotate** command to rotate the part upward as shown in Figure 4.

Figure 4

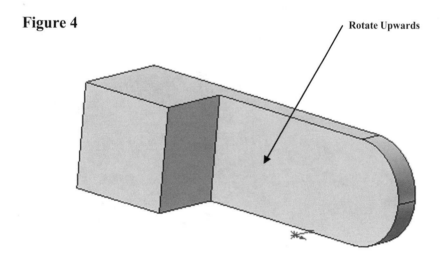

Rotate Upwards

6.   Complete the sketch as shown in Figure 5. The center of the circle is located on the corner of the fillet radius.

Figure 5

7.   Extrude the circle to a distance of **.75** inches as shown in Figure 6.

Figure 6

8.   Rotate the part around. Complete the sketch shown in Figure 7.

Figure 7

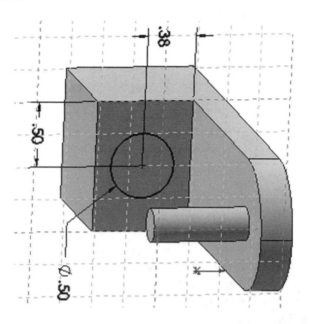

9.   Use the **Extruded Cut** option to cut a hole a distance of **1.00 inch** as shown in Figure 8.

Figure 8

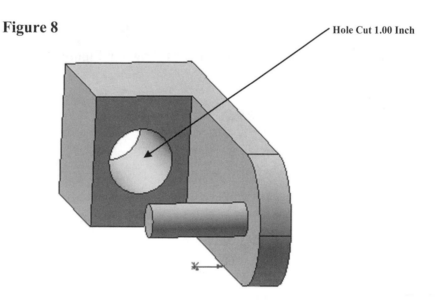

Hole Cut 1.00 Inch

10. Save the part as **Camcase1.SLDPRT** where it can be easily retrieved later.

11. Complete the sketch shown. Extrude the .500 in diameter circle to a distance of 1.00 inch and the .625 in diameter circle to a distance of .125 inches as shown in Figure 9.

Figure 9

12. The bottom of the part needs to be flat as shown in Figure 10.

Figure 10

13. Save the part as **Lifter1.SLDPRT** where it can easily be retrieved later.

14. Begin a new drawing. Complete the sketch shown in Figure 11.

Figure 11

15. Extrude the sketch to a distance of **.500** inches as shown in Figure 12.

Figure 12

.500 Inches Thick

16. Save the part as **Lobe1.SLDPRT** where it can easily be retrieved later.

17. Start a new Assembly drawing as shown in Chapter 7.

18. Move the cursor to the lower middle portion of the screen and left click on **Browse**. The Open dialog box will appear. Left click on **Camcase1.SLDPRT**. Left click on **Open** as shown in Figure 13.

Figure 13

19. SolidWorks will place one cam case in the work area. The cam case will be attached to the cursor. If the part does not appear attached to the cursor simply left click anywhere in the work area.

20. Use the **Insert Components** command to insert the **Lifter1.SLDPRT** and **Lobe1.SLDPRT** parts as shown in Figure 14.

Figure 14

21. Your screen should look similar to Figure 15.

Figure 15

22. Using the **Mate** command, place the lifter in the lifter bore as shown. You may have to change the Mate Alignment, located at the lower left portion of the screen if the lifter is mated upside down as shown in Figure 16.

Figure 16   Left Click Here If Lifter Mates Upside Down   Lifter Foot

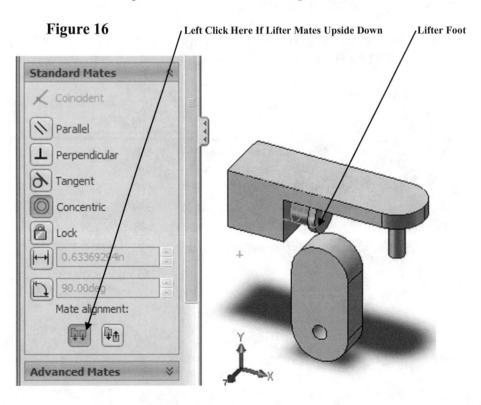

19. Rotate the assembly up as shown in Figure 17.

Figure 17

20. Use the **Mate** command to mate the lobe to the shaft as shown in Figure 18.

Figure 18

21.	Use the **Mate** command to create a **.125 inch** offset between the lobe and the case as shown in Figure 19.

Figure 19

.125 Inch Offset

22.	Use the **Rotate** command to rotate the assembly around as shown in Figure 20.

Figure 20

23. Move the cursor to the upper left portion of the screen and left click **Mate** as shown in Figure 21.

Figure 21

24. Left click on drop down arrows to the right of Mechanical Mates as shown in Figure 22.

Figure 22

25. The Mechanical Mates drop down box will appear.

26. Left click on **Cam** as shown in Figure 23.

Figure 23

Left Click Here

27. Left click on all 4 faces of the cam. You will have to rotate the assembly around (by pressing down on the mouse wheel) to gain access to all 4 faces as shown in Figure 24.

Figure 24

Left Click Here

28. Left click in the box under Cam Follower as shown in Figure 25.

Figure 25

Left Click Here

29. Left click on the Lifter foot as shown in Figure 26.

Figure 26

Left Click Here

30. SolidWorks will move the lifter down in contact with the cam face as shown in Figure 27.

Figure 27

Lifter Contacting Cam Face

Cam Follower

31. Left click on the green check mark as shown in Figure 28.

Figure 28

Left Click Here

CamMateTang...

Mates   Analysis

32. An error message will appear indicating that portions of the lobe contain a flat surface. This was done to simplify the exercise. Left click on **OK** as shown in Figure 29.

Figure 29

Left Click Here

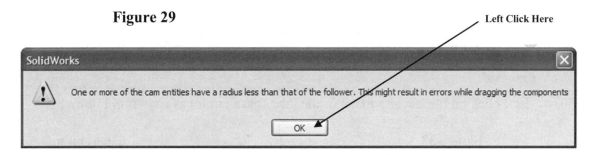

33. Move the cursor to the upper left portion of the screen and left click on the green check mark as shown in Figure 30.

Figure 30

Left Click Here

34. Move the cursor to the upper middle portion of the screen and left click on **New Motion Study** as shown in Figure 31.

Figure 31

Left Click Here

35. Left click on the **Motor** icon as shown in Figure 32.

Figure 32

Left Click Here

36. Left click on the lower portion of the lobe (base circle) as shown in Figure 33.

Figure 33

Left Click Here

37. SolidWorks will create a motor on the lower portion of the lobe as shown in Figure 34.

Figure 34

38. Move the cursor to the upper middle portion of the screen and left click on the green check mark as shown in Figure 35.

Figure 35   **Left Click Here**

39. Move the cursor to the lower left portion of the screen and left click on the Play icon as shown in Figure 36.

Figure 36   **Left Click Here**

40. Refer to Chapter 7 for more **Play** options. At this time the lifter travels out of the lifter bore. There are 2 ways to correct this. Increase the top portion of the cam case and reduce the height of the lobe. Refer to Chapter 7 on how to edit either the cam case or lobe while in the Assembly area and see the effects it would have on the system of parts. You will also notice that the lifter does not stay in contact entirely with the lobe when rotated. This is because the lobe contains 2 flat surfaces which are not typically found on a camshaft lobe.

Index